T0295730

Sustainable Innovation Reporting and Emerging Technologies

EMERALD STUDIES IN SUSTAINABLE INNOVATION MANAGEMENT

Series Editors:
Vincenzo Corvello, University of Messina, Italy
Orlando Troisi, University of Salerno, Italy

Innovation management aims to drive a repeatable, sustainable innovation process within an organization. Such initiatives focus on disruptive or step changes that transform businesses in a significant way. *Emerald Studies in Sustainable Innovation Management* considers innovation management from an interdisciplinary perspective: technological (such as digitalization) and environmental (such as green transition, energy, transportation, etc.) elements, as well as unexpected pandemics and wars that challenge innovation in both concept and practice. Volumes in this series explore scientific developments to provide new innovation principles to overcome turbulent environments, uncertainty, sustainability issues, and outdated technology.

Forthcoming Titles

Humane Entrepreneurship and Innovation: An Alternative Way to Promote Sustainable Development
By Antonio Botti and Roberto Parente

The Landscape of Innovation Intermediaries in Europe: From Theory to Practice
By Dominique Lepore

The Generative AI-Impact: Reframing Innovation in Society 5.0
Edited by Antonio Crupi, Luca Marinelli and Emanuele Cacciatore

Sustainable Innovation Reporting and Emerging Technologies: Promoting Accountability Through Artificial Intelligence, Blockchain, and the Internet of Things

BY

GENNARO MAIONE

University of Salerno, Italy

United Kingdom – North America – Japan – India – Malaysia – China

Emerald Publishing Limited
Emerald Publishing, Floor 5, Northspring, 21-23 Wellington Street, Leeds LS1 4DL

First edition 2024

Reprints and permissions service
Contact: www.copyright.com

British Library Cataloguing in Publication Data
A catalogue record for this book is available from the British Library

ISBN: 978-1-83797-740-6 (Print)
ISBN: 978-1-83797-739-0 (Online)
ISBN: 978-1-83797-741-3 (Epub)

INVESTOR IN PEOPLE

To my daughter, Alessandra.
To the freshness of her smile.
To the scent of her skin.
To the sweetness of her eyes.

A mia figlia, Alessandra.
Alla freschezza del suo sorriso.
Al profumo della sua pelle.
Alla dolcezza dei suoi occhi.

Contents

About the Author

Gennaro Maione is a researcher in Business Economics at the Department of Economics and Statistics (DISES) of the University of Salerno, Italy, where he teaches Business Administration and Accounting. He is the Guest Editor of the journal Sustainability, Topic Editor of the journal Systems, and Editorial Board Member of the Open Journal of Accounting, the Journal of Business Administration Research, the Journal of Business and Economics, the American Journal of Accounting, and the American Journal of Economics. He is the author of scientific articles presented at conferences in Italy and abroad and published in national and international journals. His main research interests focus on accounting and accountability and include sustainability, the environment, and technological innovation.

Preface

Amidst the intricate fabric of human pursuits, the communal yearning for a world that functions harmoniously encounters the relentless progress of nascent technological breakthroughs, which entice us toward unexplored domains and challenge established socioeconomic frameworks. In exploring the nexus of innovation, sustainability, technology, and accounting, the book weaves a narrative transcending disciplinary boundaries and fostering awareness of humanity's shared responsibilities.

The fundamental inquiry of this work resides in the acknowledgment of a novel construal of accounting, which was formerly perceived as a mere mirror of economic transactions but has since burgeoned into an influence that molds the essence of human existence. The Greek philosopher Heraclitus wisely observed that "all entities move, and nothing remains still." In this perpetual motion and relentless evolution spirit, this book explores sustainable innovation reporting, seeking to forge new paths and enrich human understanding by answering the following three research questions (RQs).

RQ1. To what extent did the historical transformation of accounting, from a passive reflection of economic transactions to an active force shaping our societal fabric, affect the trajectory of sustainable innovation reporting?

RQ2. In light of the progression outlining the worldwide accounting domain, what are the predictable obstacles and prospects that await sustainable innovation reporting?

RQ3. How can accounting scholars and practitioners converge to create synergies, exchange knowledge, and contribute to the ongoing discourse on sustainable innovation reporting to foster transparency, accountability, and ethical conduct within organizations?

With five thought-provoking chapters on various aspects of sustainable innovation reporting, this work promotes the realization of accountability through the implementation of emerging technologies.

Chapter 1 sheds light on the origins of accounting thought, sustainable innovation reporting principles, and technological advancements' transformative potential. The historical, ethical, and philosophical foundations of accounting and accountability-innovation relationships are examined. This chapter examines the history of accounting thought, from double-entry bookkeeping to the modern discipline and the rise of sustainability and social responsibility.

It concludes by considering the paradox of control and flexibility, risk-taking and technological advancement, the complex equilibrium between conventional accounting principles and innovative approaches, and stakeholder expectations at the accountability-innovation nexus.

Chapter 2 expounds on the multifaceted interconnection between ethical facets, transparency, trust, and the influence of technology on accounting and accountability. The historical roots of ethical principles, professional conduct, decision-making, and corporate governance are debated. Questing for an ethically accountable culture, this chapter also examines the repercussions of unethical practices on stakeholders and the role of accounting education and professional development in molding ethical values.

Subsequently, the discussion moves toward highlighting the possibilities of emerging technologies in promoting openness and overcoming the obstacles that arise due to the lack of trustworthiness and reliability within the accounting industry. Afterward, the discourse focuses on ethical reporting and methodologies, accentuating the pivotal role of cross-disciplinary research on accounting ethics. This chapter closes by examining the role of accounting bodies and regulators in light of the evolution of professional standards.

Chapter 3 dives into the nuances surrounding accounting applications powered by Artificial Intelligence (AI). It contemplates ethical deliberations on data privacy, security, algorithmic bias, and impartiality. Subsequently, the discourse shifts toward the obligations of professional organizations and regulatory bodies to guarantee the ethical execution of AI-driven accounting practices.

This chapter culminates in a case study, illustrating the intersection between AI and sustainable innovation reporting. The analysis delves into the results and best practices of actual implementation, thereby providing a tangible representation of this convergence.

Chapter 4 focuses on the impact of blockchain technology on sustainable innovation reporting. At first, the underpinnings of blockchain in accounting are unfolded to delve into the theoretical foundations elucidating the transformative potential of this technology, including double-entry bookkeeping, triple-entry accounting systems, and the ramifications of information asymmetry and Agency theory in blockchain-based accounting.

This chapter discusses the pivotal function of stakeholder engagement in decentralized accountability mechanisms. It also provides insight into the revolutionary capacity of blockchain as a stimulant for trust and transparency in accounting. Finally, a case study shows how blockchain technology promotes decentralized accountability.

Chapter 5 examines the connection between the Internet of Things (IoT) and sustainable innovation reporting to investigate how the former could change accounting and society. An overview of how IoT is reconfiguring the modus operandi of accounting experts in terms of data-centric discernment and judgment is proposed to outline the limitless prospects for solutions that this technology offers while also underscoring the significance of embracing a human-centric approach to propel the causes of sustainable preservation and ethical responsibility. Ultimately, a case study analysis shows how IoT may affect the reporting of sustainable innovation while also considering its possible hazards associated with digital inclusion and access, standardization, and interoperability issues.

Given these premises, this book is intended to act as a boost for thoughtful reflection and transformative action. May the stimuli gleaned from these pages inspire the reader to join the quest for sustainable innovation and contribute to the ongoing discourse on promoting accountability through emerging technologies.

Thus, with great enthusiasm and profound humility, I welcome you to "Sustainable Innovation Reporting and Emerging Technologies: promoting Accountability through Artificial Intelligence, Blockchain, and the Internet of Things."

The author
Gennaro Maione

Chapter 1

Conceptualizing Sustainable Innovation Reporting in the Age of Technological Advancements

1.1 The Foundations of Sustainable Innovation Reporting

The study of accounting foundations reveals the progression of human civilization's socioeconomic customs. Seeking knowledge in this field implies exploring the intricacies of the past and uncovering the origins of sustainable innovation reporting (Maione et al., 2023a, 2023b). This discipline originated from converging ancient accounting traditions, double-entry bookkeeping, ecological, societal, and administrative considerations, and technological advances (Bebbington & Larrinaga, 2014).

Accounting procedures played a significant role in society's management and business throughout history; the papyrus ledgers of Egypt and the prehistoric clay tablets from Sumeria attest to the discipline's continued relevance.

The Italian Renaissance introduced double-entry bookkeeping, revolutionizing modern accounting (Soll, 2014). Industrialization and modernization fostered the development of several accounting theories and approaches, requiring regulatory organizations and standards (Nobes et al., 2008). This strengthened accounting's position as a worldwide economic pillar (Maione, 2023).

With the advent of the new millennium, the call for sustainability and corporate social responsibility (CSR) started reverberating among the clamor for expansion and advancement, stimulating a moral awareness that organizations must be stewards of our future (Gray & Milne, 2018).

Sustainable innovation reporting has progressively developed as an area of study to address the complicated relationship between accounting practices, social and environmental issues, and the transformational potential of technology (Eccles & Serafeim, 2014; Tommasetti, Mussari, et al., 2020). This trend inspired new accounting approaches and frameworks to link financial performance with environmental, social, and governance (ESG) goals (Adams & Larrinaga, 2019).

For some years, emerging technologies, such as artificial intelligence (AI), blockchain, and the Internet of Things (IoT), have been transforming accounting

Sustainable Innovation Reporting and Emerging Technologies, 1–13
Copyright © 2024 Gennaro Maione
Published under exclusive licence by Emerald Publishing Limited
doi:10.1108/978-1-83797-739-020241001

(Appelbaum et al., 2017; Lytras et al., 2019; Lytras & Visvizi, 2018, 2021). This has resulted in an augmentation of accuracy and efficacy in traditional methodologies while facilitating the dissemination of sustainable innovation reports through novel conduits (Cohen & Simnett, 2018). The connection between these technological advancements and sustainable innovation reporting opened up a new horizon in accounting scholarship, stimulating innovative contemplation and reflection (Busco, Frigo, Quattrone, et al., 2013).

1.1.1 Key Principles and Values of Sustainable Innovation Reporting

In the vast domain of accounting thought, sustainable innovation reporting emerges as a multifaceted endeavor, seeking to weave together the threads of sustainability, innovation, and accountability in reporting procedures. The principles and values of sustainable innovation reporting include materiality, relevance, completeness, accuracy, transparency, clarity, comparability, and consistency.

Materiality refers to determining which aspects hold particular pertinence and influence in depicting an organization's value-creation process. In sustainable innovation, materiality assumes a significantly elevated role in shaping the fabric of an organization's disclosures (Eccles & Serafeim, 2013; Milne & Gray, 2013). In light of the nature of sustainable innovation, materiality is an instrumental paradigm for effectively navigating the diverse spectrum of stakeholder demands and conflicting objectives. The complex relationship between materiality and its amalgamation with ecological responsibility and novelty is pivotal in constructing a fabric that accurately mirrors a corporation's strategic goals and achievements (Adams, 2015).

The notion of relevance is linked to the idea that disclosed information must possess the power to influence the decision-making processes of its intended audience. Within the context of sustainable innovation, it assumes a heightened significance, shaping the contours of the narrative that elucidates an organization's strategic endeavors and performance in sustainability (Unerman & Zappettini, 2014). The practice of relevance invites practitioners to engage in an ongoing dialogue between the organization and its stakeholders to ensure the faithful representation of the journey toward sustainable value creation (Adams et al., 2016).

The focal point of completeness depicts organizations' efficacy, encompassing all notable facets across the economic, social, and environmental domains. Completeness guarantees that no salient aspects of an organization's operations are neglected or downplayed, affording stakeholders a more comprehensive understanding of the organization's undertakings and ramifications.

The attainment of completeness entails contemplating not solely the present undertakings of the organization but also how these may metamorphose in the future owing to strategic realignments, developing market circumstances, or shifting societal norms. Moreover, completeness implies that organizations should provide a well-rounded depiction of their conduct's favorable and unfavorable consequences. This necessitates accentuating accomplishments and positive contributions and recognizing and confronting obstacles, defeats, and adverse effects of the actions undertaken.

Accuracy is founded upon the principle that information divulged ought to be veracious and precise, devoid of inaccuracies or distortions. It requires technical accuracy and impartial, comprehensive reporting of the organization's efforts, successes, and impacts.

Accuracy involves data presentation without bias or misrepresentation to avoid incorrect conclusions or assumptions. To achieve sustainable innovation, organizations must use sustainable business models, technologies, and practices (Deegan, 2017). To help stakeholders understand their sustainability performance, organizations must clearly and accurately explain their goals and methods (Cho et al., 2015).

Transparency lies in the complete and unequivocal revelation of relevant data, cultivating an environment of reliance and answerability between organizations and their diverse interested parties (Maione et al., 2022). Within sustainable innovation, transparency guarantees that an organization's sustainability is communicated in all aspects (Christensen et al., 2017; Crane & Matten, 2010).

Transparency embodies the virtue of forthrightly revealing knowledge that may affect the interests of a given organization's stakeholders. In pursuing sustainable innovation, transparency emerges as a pivotal element in an organization's communication strategy, guaranteeing that its sustainability efforts are revealed in an all-encompassing way.

Clarity is central to determining what constitutes lucid and comprehensible information (Laine et al., 2021; Unerman et al., 2021). It pertains to conveying information, emphasizing simplicity and accessibility for all parties involved. Obtaining clarity demands abstaining from using ambiguous terminology or a lexicon that may obscure the intended communication or deceive the recipients (Farneti & Guthrie, 2009; Solomons, 1991). Within sustainable innovation, clarity connotes the capacity for diverse stakeholders to readily comprehend an organization's sustainability endeavors and their resultant effects (Rimmel & Jonäll, 2013). This favors discernment in decision-making, participation by all parties, and accountability. To ensure that knowledge is accessible, meaningful, and applicable, clarity is crucial (Flower, 2015).

The concept of comparability pertains to the capacity to gauge and juxtapose organizational performance across temporal intervals (Cho et al., 2015). It facilitates the comprehension of stakeholders regarding the advancement of an organization's sustainability endeavors and their comparison with the established benchmarks or paradigms of the industry (Unerman et al., 2021).

The attainment of comparability necessitates the implementation of uniform gauges and criteria that are consistently applied across various establishments and temporal dimensions (Flower, 2015). The act of assessing advancement, recognizing the best methodologies, and promoting comparative analysis and knowledge acquisition can greatly assist (Lozano, 2013). Moreover, the comparability concept bestows stakeholders with the ability to exercise informed judgment (Eccles & Serafeim, 2014).

Consistency in accounting and reporting is predicated upon an unyielding dedication to utilizing coherent methodologies and protocols throughout a specified period. The principle in question is paramount: ensuring the reliability and uniformity of data and information (Lozano, 2013).

In sustainable innovation, preserving constancy is critical to establishing an organization's sustainability reporting as a dependable source of knowledge (Laine et al., 2021). It facilitates the execution of longitudinal scrutiny and comparative evaluation, thereby augmenting the general equilibrium and permanence of the organization (Cho et al., 2015). The consistency principle also enlightens stakeholders regarding the trends and patterns in an organization's sustainability performance (Flower, 2015).

1.2 Emerging Technologies in Accounting Scholarship: AI, Blockchain, and the IoT

Throughout the chronicles of the accounting discipline, the unrelenting advancement of society has observed the revolutionary influence of emerging technologies on the bedrock tenets and methodologies of the field (Maione & Leoni, 2021). The unstoppable wave of technological advancement gave rise to a diverse range of tools transforming the terrain of accounting academia (Appelbaum et al., 2017), including AI, blockchain, and IoT.

AI is leading these emerging technologies because it combines computational methods that give machines human-like reasoning, learning, and perception (Russell & Norvig, 2016). Machine learning and natural language processing have revolutionized financial analysis, risk management, and auditing (Janvrin et al., 2014) and are among the AI subfields that hold particular relevance for accounting (Leoni et al., 2021; Maione & Leoni, 2021).

Delving into the array of AI's manifold accounting applications, we notice many revolutionary innovations. From machine learning algorithms to turn complex financial data into actionable insights to natural language processing to decipher regulatory texts and financial reports, AI will transform accounting.

Similarly, blockchain technology promises to instigate a transformative shift in accounting by enhancing and streamlining various processes and operations, such as recording, authentication, and disclosing financial data. The advent of this technological breakthrough, founded upon the deployment of a decentralized, immutable, and transparent digital ledger, is presently engendering noteworthy prospects within the discipline of accounting.

Its scope of influence spans a broad range of functions, including the monitoring of assets, the secure conveyance of data, and the fortification of audit trails (Dai & Vasarhelyi, 2017). This technology presents manifold challenges and opportunities for both accounting practitioners and scholars. The promise of enhanced transparency, security, and efficiency beckons, yet the road ahead is fraught with uncertainty and the weight of uncharted territory (Alderman & Jollineau, 2020).

In the triptych of emerging technologies shaping new and innovative accounting scholarship, the IoT has the potential to revolutionize financial information collection, computation, and evaluation (Mattern & Floerkemeier, 2010). IoT advances include instantaneous financial information acquisition, automated inventory supervision (Li et al., 2016), and asset monitoring (Atzori et al., 2010).

1.3 The Accountability–Innovation Gap

The accountability–innovation gap illustrates the complex relationship between two seemingly opposing forces in accounting. Understanding this gap implies deepening the intricacies of reconciling accountability and innovation, scrutinizing the paradoxical interplay between control and flexibility, the reluctance to embrace change, and the persistence of organizational inertia. It also requires examining the potential synergies that can be leveraged to augment sustainable innovation reporting.

The interdependent correlation between accountability and innovation underscores the mutual influence of these notions, whereby accountability serves as a guiding principle for innovative methodologies while innovation propels advancements in accountability. The link between various aspects of accounting demands a nuanced equilibrium between upholding conventional principles and promoting inventive methods.

The challenge of reconciling control and flexibility and surmounting resistance to change and organizational inertia engenders challenges and prospects for achieving such an equilibrium. Identifying strategies to manage this challenge is pivotal in enabling organizations to cultivate a culture that values accountability and innovation.

Additionally, studying accountability and innovation may help create a framework that effectively integrates these concepts. This would help accounting move forward and create more value while making reporting on sustainable innovation easier.

1.3.1 The Relationship Between Accountability and Innovation

The accounting discipline is situated at a fascinating crossroads where the concepts of accountability and innovation engage in a dialectical interplay, mutually influencing and propelling progress within the domain. The interdependent correlation between accountability and innovation within accounting is paramount to preserving the discipline's authenticity while accommodating a constantly evolving environment (Busco, Frigo, & Riccaboni, 2013).

Accountability assumes a crucial position in the advancement and execution of pioneering methodologies. It serves as a rudimentary structure of norms and doctrines that upholds the authenticity and reliability of financial data in the face of any plausible breach. Contrarily, it can be argued that the driving force behind innovation is to promote the progression of accountability by ushering in novel methodologies and technologies that enhance accounting practices' effectiveness, accuracy, and clarity (Haller & van Staden, 2014).

Balancing accounting norms with innovation is challenging (Ezzamel et al., 2007). To achieve equilibrium, accounting practices must combine novelty with accountability. A flexible mindset, a corporate culture that embraces change, and technological innovations to improve accounting methods are needed to adapt to the ever-changing business environment (Christensen & Raynor, 2013).

Novelty and advancement require some risk-taking, which may conflict with accounting methodology accountability (Knechel & Willekens, 2006). The interaction between innovation and accounting practices necessitates implementing proficient risk management strategies. The performance of a sturdy risk management framework enables organizations to recognize, evaluate, and alleviate the hazards that are linked with pioneering pursuits, thus achieving a harmonious balance between venturing into uncertainty and being accountable for the consequences of such actions (Tekathen & Dechow, 2013).

The influence of stakeholder expectations on the equilibrium between accountability and innovation in accounting practices is of paramount significance. Given the elevated demands of stakeholders for transparency, accuracy, and efficiency in financial reporting and disclosure, the accounting community has to face the arduous task of harmonizing potential contradictions between the quest for novelty and the unwavering commitment to established tenets of accountability. Participation in innovation can help stakeholders align their expectations with accounting practices, promoting a mutually beneficial balance between accountability and innovation (Gray, 2002).

1.3.1.1 The Interdependence of Accountability and Innovation

The connection between accountability and innovation within the accounting domain is profoundly enmeshed within the very fabric of the discipline (Brown & Dillard, 2015). Considering the historical, philosophical, and empirical aspects of accounting may help to attain a comprehensive understanding of this complex interrelation.

The progression of accounting over time was characterized by a perpetual interplay between the exigencies of accountability and the impetus of innovation (Zeff, 2015). Accounting practices emerged to meet the demands of more complex financial transactions. According to Soll (2014), the principles of accountability are essential to ensure that these novel practices align with ethical standards and promote transparency. Innovation engendered the evolution of novel instruments and methodologies that amplified the accounting profession's aptitude to cater to the requisites of burgeoning economies (Carmona & Trombetta, 2008). This ongoing interaction between accountability and innovation persisted throughout the centuries, shaping the trajectory of accounting as we know it today (Zeff, 2015).

Dialectical reasoning can help understand the complex relationship between accountability and innovation. The Hegelian dialectic method combines opposing and seemingly incompatible elements like the thesis and antithesis to advance knowledge and understanding (Hegel, 1807). When we apply this theoretical conception to accounting, we can discern that accountability is the thesis, while innovation assumes the antithesis role. Incorporating these ostensibly contradictory forces begets a more resilient and versatile accounting discipline proficient in tackling the requisites of a swiftly transforming terrain (Boland et al., 2008).

Empirical evidence confirms the existence of a profound interconnectedness between accountability and innovation. Gendron et al. (2007) found that pioneering performance measurement systems like the Balanced Scorecard increased accountability by providing a more comprehensive framework for assessing organizational performance. Granlund and Lukka (2017) consistently expound that adopting novel accounting information systems engendered a heightened sense of responsibility by augmenting the efficacy and precision of financial reporting.

The close connection between accountability and innovation significantly impacts the accounting discipline's response to unprecedented challenges like the emergence of AI, blockchain technology, and IoT (Brynjolfsson & McAfee, 2014). Given the impact of these groundbreaking advancements on traditional accounting methodologies, this discipline must consider the ethical and pragmatic implications of emerging technology integration (Hysa et al., 2022; Kokina et al., 2017; Kruja et al., 2019).

1.3.1.2 The Balance Between Traditional Accounting Principles and Innovative Approaches

The pursuit of balance between conventional principles of accounting and novel approaches necessitates profound contemplation of the influence of technology, which arose as an essential power in determining the destiny of the accounting profession. The accounting discipline is pressured to engage with technological advancement's ethical and practical ramifications in light of its extensive effects, particularly in AI, blockchain, and IoT (Appelbaum et al., 2017).

This discourse revolves around the deep-seated influence that technology wields over the underlying tenets of accounting. The combination of sophisticated tools and methodologies risks upsetting the customary mores and conventions that the profession has followed for a long time. To adequately confront this pressing matter, accounting scholars and practitioners must engage in a comprehensive and reflective process to thoroughly examine the fundamental assumptions and principles woven into the fabric of conventional accounting doctrines and modern technological advancements (Janvrin et al., 2014).

Due to technological advancement, the accounting profession must be proactive and vigilant about ethical issues (Kokina et al., 2017). Recognizing the societal and ethical duties intrinsic to the accounting profession embodies a crucial ethical archetype that must be maintained to preserve the genuineness and dependability of accounting methodologies amidst the extensive changes of our time (Gendron et al., 2007).

Balancing conventional accounting doctrines and cutting-edge techniques requires a complex and nuanced strategy (Beattie, 2014). Pursuing technological progress necessitates a delicate balance between integrating novel methodologies within established convictions, establishing an environment that fosters perpetual learning and cogitation, and contemplating the moral implications of technological advancement (Barth, 2015).

The quest for knowledge and its pragmatic application present a captivating prospect for fostering synergistic alliances between accounting scholars and professionals, encompassing information technology, administration, and ethics (Appelbaum et al., 2017). Engaging in collaborative endeavors can be a powerful catalyst for generating innovative ideas and enhancing the accounting discourse surrounding the equilibrium between conventional approaches and cutting-edge methodologies (Haller & van Staden, 2014).

1.3.1.3 The Tension Between Risk-Taking and Accountability

The relationship between venturing into uncertainty and assuming accountability epitomizes the essence of innovative endeavor (Malsch & Gendron, 2013). The coexistence of a fundamental dichotomy in engaging in innovative methodologies while concurrently upholding ethical and professional principles underscores the intricate equilibrium that must be achieved. The attainment of this equilibrium necessitates a comprehensive scrutiny of the fundamental forces at play (Boland et al., 2008).

Taking risks to explore new territory, challenge norms, and embrace uncertainty to solve complex problems requires boldness (Simnett & Huggins, 2015). In accounting, this can materialize through pioneering methodologies, avant-garde technologies, and innovative reporting frameworks. The advent of these novel advancements harbors the possibility of a transformative impact on the conventions of the accounting profession, thereby amplifying its capacity to conform to the incessantly evolving requisites of a changing society (Christensen et al., 2017).

Accountability concerns accountants' ethical and professional obligation to ensure the information's transparency, adequacy, and correctness (Gray et al., 1996). This concept counterbalances the human tendency toward heedlessness and promotes a culture of obligation that safeguards the genuineness and soundness of accounting techniques (Malsch & Gendron, 2013).

The relationship between the inclination toward risk-taking and accountability can be perceived as a manifestation of the broader discourse between the principles of innovation and established traditions. Risk management balances risk-taking and accountability (Haller & van Staden, 2014).

Risk management, which uses a systematic and forward-thinking approach to identify, assess, and mitigate risks and opportunities, may bridge the desire to create a moral obligation. A balance between novelty and caution in accounting practices can lead to flexible and robust methods (Simnett & Huggins, 2015).

The tension between uncharted paths and accountability requires deeply examining innovation's potential effects on society (Boland et al., 2008; Malsch & Gendron, 2013).

1.3.1.4 The Impact of Stakeholder Expectations on the Accountability–Innovation Nexus

Stakeholder expectations significantly impact the interplay between accountability and innovation in the accounting profession. These expectations shape customs, benchmarks, and protocols that balance innovation and caution (Boland et al., 2008; Malsch & Gendron, 2013). Changing stakeholder expectations requires the accounting profession to maintain its credibility and adaptability to global business demands (Deegan, 2002; Donaldson & Preston, 1995; Unerman & Bennett, 2004).

The stakeholder theory explains how stakeholder expectations affect accountability and innovation (Freeman et al., 2010; Gray et al., 1996). Their quest for ethical and pragmatic excellence posits that organizations are profoundly responsible for cultivating and nurturing their relationships with stakeholders by duly recognizing and attending to their rightful aspirations and apprehensions (Donaldson & Preston, 1995; Mitchell ct al., 1997).

One of the pivotal facets of stakeholder expectations pertains to the yearning for augmented transparency, reliability, and consistency in financial reporting.

The proposition above entails the imperative need to establish resilient and consistent principles and techniques of bookkeeping (Barth, 2015; Eccles & Krzus, 2010). The discipline's unwavering emphasis on accountability, which promotes conservatism and adherence to long-standing norms and principles, may slow innovation (Malsch & Gendron, 2013).

Due to stakeholders' expectations, the profession may and must adapt to rapidly changing technological, economic, and social contexts (Busch et al., 2016). The rise of ESG reporting shows stakeholders' changing views of accounting's role in sustainable development and problem-solving (Eccles et al., 2014). The cultivation of stakeholder expectations catalyzes the accounting profession to embrace avant-garde methodologies, tools, and reporting frameworks that augment both pertinence and worth within a convoluted global economic, social, and environmental milieu (Christensen et al., 2017; Simnett & Huggins, 2015).

The accounting profession's complex sociopolitical, cultural, and institutional frameworks shape stakeholders' expectations. As explained by Hopwood (2009) and Cooper et al. (2017), the complex web of interconnected forces shapes the very fabric of the accounting profession. Comprehending stakeholder expectations and the interplay between accountability and innovation is multifaceted. It requires the analysis of interrelated elements, encompassing regulatory frameworks, professional standards, organizational cultures, and technological advancements (Malsch & Gendron, 2013).

1.3.2 Challenges and Opportunities in Balancing Accountability and Innovation

Understanding the relationship between control and flexibility, strong resistance to change and organizational inertia, and accountability and innovation can reveal many strategies and frameworks to help the accounting profession fulfill its many responsibilities in a changing global landscape.

The challenge of reconciling the imperative of upholding control and conformity to established accounting norms with the need for adaptability and originality presents a paradox (Otley, 2016).

The resolution of this paradox necessitates the discernment of tactics that govern duality and cultivate an equitable method to answerability and ingenuity, lessening probable conflicts and encouraging harmonious prospects (Farneti & Guthrie, 2009).

Change and organizational inertia can disrupt the delicate balance between accountability and innovation in accounting (Burns & Scapens, 2000). It is essential to put forth methodologies that transcend the obstacles and foster a mindset that values responsibility and originality, empowering the discipline to acclimate and flourish on a perpetually transforming path (Busco, Frigo, Quattrone, et al., 2013).

A thorough examination of the possible harmonization between accountability and innovation in propelling advancement and the generation of worth in accounting presents auspicious paths for forthcoming inquiry and implementation (Christensen et al., 2017).

Through the proposition of a comprehensive structure that harmoniously amalgamates accountability and innovation, we may ultimately improve the reporting of sustainable innovation and make a valuable contribution to the advancement of the accounting profession (Busch et al., 2016).

1.3.2.1 The Paradox of Control and Flexibility

At the heart of the pursuit to reconcile accountability and innovation in accounting lies the paradox of control and flexibility (Otley, 2016). Conventional accounting principles require strict adherence to rules, making it harder to develop innovative ideas (Adler & Borys, 1996; Hopwood, 2009).

The accounting discipline implements strict norms, statutes, and methods to ensure financial data accuracy, dependability, and uniformity (Nobes et al., 2008). Control emphasis strengthens the profession's ability to provide decision-relevant knowledge to various interested parties (Henderson et al., 2015; Watts & Zimmerman, 1986). However, flexibility is essential to innovation. It transcends rigidity, embraces change, and triggers new ideas and discoveries, fostering progress.

To resolve this apparent contradiction, companies and accountants should adopt adaptable organizational structures, develop and use flexible skills, and use current, principle-based accounting standards. This would help organizations and accountants balance control and flexibility, resulting in a fairer and more balanced relationship between accountability and innovation (Farneti & Guthrie, 2009).

Resilient organizational structures can provide control and flexibility (Gibson & Birkinshaw, 2004; O'Reilly & Tushman, 2004; Simsek et al., 2009). Companies can stay true to their financial principles while encouraging "new" ideas by setting up systems for ideation and government oversight (Smith & Tushman, 2005). The repeated oscillation between the two dimensions guarantees advancement (Lavie et al., 2010).

Another option is cross-functional teams with diverse backgrounds and expertise (Jansen et al., 2009; Tushman & O'Reilly, 1996). Organizations should invest in skill development and a resilience-promoting culture (Gibson & Birkinshaw, 2004). This implies cultivating an environment that stimulates cooperation, education, and exploration, all while upholding a steadfast commitment to conformity and the observance of established accounting principles. In light of this, the organization's members must be endowed with the authority to partake in the innovation process while simultaneously fulfilling their obligation to ensure accountability (Rogan & Mors, 2014).

An organization can restructure and adapt its resources and competencies to changing business conditions with dynamic capabilities (Teece et al., 1997). To develop dynamic accounting skills, you must improve methods, procedures, and frameworks to balance accountability and innovation.

In accounting, making sense of things through a social construction of reality is crucial for spotting new patterns, opportunities, and problems (Teece, 2007). If stakeholders' needs, the law, technology change, or other conditions vary, organizations must monitor their surroundings and adapt to the change (Abernethy & Stoelwinder, 1995). Organizations can maintain their position at the forefront of innovation by anticipating and responding proactively to the constantly changing environment thanks to their increased awareness, which Weick et al. (2005) outlined as upholding the principles of accountability.

Additionally, Sirmon et al. (2007) emphasized the importance of developing an organization's capacity to recognize opportunities through resource orchestration. Adequate human, financial, and technological capital distribution helps innovation projects while maintaining control and compliance infrastructure (Teece, 2007).

According to Helfat and Peteraf (2003), the skillful coordination of resources enables organizations to engage in groundbreaking endeavors consistent with their strategic goals and the larger accountability framework. Teece et al. (1997) state that the dynamic capabilities to change and adapt existing structures, processes, and systems to meet society's ever-changing needs are most important. Companies may need to change how they share information, adopt new technology, or restructure their teams to encourage creativity while maintaining strong regulation (Eisenhardt & Martin, 2000). Organizations must constantly improve and adapt these factors to meet changing accountability and innovation needs (Jansen et al., 2009).

Implementing principle-based accounting standards gives organizations a solid foundation for harmonizing accountability and innovation. Zeff (2015) suggests a flexible framework that emphasizes accounting's core principles and goals instead of strict rules. Accounting standards improve understanding of the field's fundamental goals and rules (Benston et al., 2006), efficiency (Herath & Richardson, 2018), job performance, and decision-making.

1.3.2.2 The Resistance to Change and Organizational Inertia

A complex web of traditions and customs has been kept alive and improved in accounting (Covaleski et al., 1993). Any attempt to change customs and conventions may provoke resistance and reluctance to new ideas (Hopper & Major, 2007). Resistance to change and organizational inertia hinder innovation (Burns & Scapens, 2000). Resistant habits, societal norms, conventions, or fear of the potential negative consequences of change can hinder change (Armenakis & Bedeian, 1999; Battilana & Casciaro, 2012; Ezzamel et al., 2007; Nelson & Winter, 1985).

This is also true in accounting (Dillard et al., 2004), where encouraging conversation and sharing ideas is a key way to get people to accept change and create a healthy balance between responsibility and new ideas. Organizations can promote a way of life that values diversity, encourages service, and strengthens the pursuit of innovative methodologies by encouraging open and transparent communication (Carmeli et al., 2010; Edmondson, 2003).

These methodologies include meetings, workshops, focus groups (Maurer, 2010), and platforms that promote an environment of emotional safety, a crucial component in progress (Nembhard & Edmondson, 2006). Organizations can also use digital communication tools and remote work arrangements to encourage idea sharing (Hinds & Kiesler, 2002). Through collaborative software, social media, or intranets, individuals can expeditiously exchange knowledge, perceptions, and concepts, cultivating continuous education and advancement (Alavi & Leidner, 2001). In this case, the employment of digital platforms transcends their customary function, as they can function as a conduit for disseminating knowledge about organizational alterations. This practice may encourage transparency and interdependence in the workplace (Treem & Leonardi, 2013).

Organizations must establish feedback channels to hear and implement employee feedback (Anseel et al., 2015). Implementing tools such as suggestion boxes, periodic employee surveys, or anonymous reporting mechanisms can be a viable remedy (Detert & Edmondson, 2011).

Companies can also include staff in decision-making to overcome change resistance and balance accountability and innovation. Participating in decision-making can inspire deep change in an organization. Cross-functional teams are another good way to reduce resistance to change and organizational inertia (Parker & Axtell, 2001). Putting together groups of people from different fields within a company can help build collective expertise and encourage creativity in creating and using accounting protocols and methods (Bunderson & Sutcliffe, 2003). In addition, such teams can help organizations understand their goals and constraints, leading to more effective and ethical solutions (Denison et al., 1996).

Consensus-based decision-making protocols may promote harmony and cooperation (Susskind & Cruikshank, 1987). Consensus-driven decision-making can help companies identify potential obstacles, address employee concerns, and foster a shared commitment to change. To this aim, Group Decision Support Systems (GDSS) are widely employed for consensus-driven decision-making, allowing organizations to tap into their employees' ingenuity using computer tools, unleashing great potential and leading to innovation and progress (DeSanctis & Gallupe, 1987).

Empathetic and supportive leadership is another decisive factor for overcoming change resistance and balancing accountability and innovation. It engenders an environment in which they feel motivated to participate in the progression of the organization's methodologies (Bass & Avolio, 1994). This type of leadership is crucial for breaking down barriers (Graen & Uhl-Bien, 1995). Communicating a compelling vision, supporting ambitious goals, and providing individual support and encouragement motivates subordinates (Bass, 1985). Leaders can empower employees to express their thoughts and feelings by promoting psychological safety. This approach has the potential to successfully alleviate resistance toward change and foster a more holistic and innovative method of generating innovation (Bono & Judge, 2004).

Drafting change management protocols is another way to deal with change resistance, balance, regulation, and flexibility (Kotter, 1996). Well-planned change management protocols help organizations handle accounting transformation challenges and unknowns, boosting flexibility, creativity, and responsibility (Burnes, 2004).

Chapter 2

Ethical Imperatives for Sustainable Innovation Reporting

2.1 The Historical Evolution of Ethics in Accounting

The ethical fabric of the accounting discipline withstood the trials of time, adapting to cater to society's changing requisites and expectations. Since antiquity, religious and cultural factors have shaped the normative framework that governed financial affairs and records, which led to ethical considerations in accounting.

Ancient societies like Mesopotamia, Egypt, and Greece linked accounting's ontological foundations to their theological and cultural norms (Mattessich, 2003). The Code of Hammurabi, for example, placed paramount importance on the fairness of transactions, with particular provisions devoted to subjects such as usurious interest rates. The Greek philosophers Aristotle and Plato emphasized the importance of ethical principles in business, praising temperance and equity in financial dealings (Matten & Moon, 2004).

Medieval accounting ethics emphasized spiritual values, particularly Christianity and Islam, advocating the importance of integrity, rectitude, and conscientiousness in commercial dealings. During this time, moral discussions played a major role in shaping the development of accounting methods, including the start of the Islamic way of keeping ledgers (Mirakhor & Askari, 2010).

The spread of the Roman Catholic Church across Europe helped establish ecclesiastical bookkeeping methods, which promoted ethical principles like accountability and transparency in canonical financial management (Edwards, 1989). Monastic orders developed double-entry bookkeeping, which was the basis for modern accounting practices, demonstrating the medieval ecclesiastical influence on ethical standards in accounting (Yamey, 1949).

The emergence of double-entry bookkeeping during the 15th century by Luca Pacioli marked the inception of contemporary accounting (Sangster, 2016). As the intricacy of financial transactions increased and companies proliferated, a compelling necessity emerged for more resilient and uniform accounting methodologies (Baker & Bettner, 1997).

Sustainable Innovation Reporting and Emerging Technologies, 15–27
Copyright © 2024 Gennaro Maione
Published under exclusive licence by Emerald Publishing Limited
doi:10.1108/978-1-83797-739-020241002

During the early modern period, accounting treatises emerged, including Pacioli's "Summa de Arithmetica, Geometria, Proportioni et Proportionalita" and Dafforne's "The Merchant's Mirror." These works examined bookkeeping and accounting ethics (Geijsbeek, 1914), laying the groundwork for ethical considerations in modern theory and practice.

Over the 19th century, the Generally Accepted Accounting Principles (GAAP) were progressively outlined. The American Institute of Certified Public Accountants (AICPA) and the Institute of Chartered Accountants in England and Wales (ICAEW) were founded (Brown & Dillard, 2014). The rise of industrialization throughout the 19th and 20th centuries catalyzed the progression of accounting theory due to the heightened complexities and interrelatedness of companies and economies. In this period, novel accounting ideologies and techniques emerged, including cost accounting, management accounting, and financial statement analysis (Nobes & Parker, 2008). A sequence of financial disasters culminated in the epochal Great Depression, reinforcing the criticality of ethical deliberations in accounting methodologies. Events during this time led to the creation of rules meant to improve transparency and give investors confidence by setting standards for accounting and auditing (Previts & Merino, 1979).

Accounting scandals in subsequent decades underscored the importance of ethical conduct and heightened the call for regulatory reforms and professional supervision (Arnold & De Lange, 2004). Financial crises engendered the necessity for the creation of two new regulatory bodies: the Financial Accounting Standards Board (FASB) and the Public Company Accounting Oversight Board (PCAOB) (Arens et al., 2010).

During the 1900s, a growing emphasis was placed on CSR and sustainability reporting as companies became progressively cognizant of their ethical duties to diverse stakeholders, encompassing personnel, customers, and the ecosystem (Gray et al., 1996; Owen, 2005). The advent of sustainability and CSR emphasized the propagation of social and environmental responsibility alongside financial transparency (Deegan, 2002; Del Bene, Tommasetti, Leoni, et al., 2020; Del Bene, Tommasetti, Maione, et al., 2020).

The scandals in the early 21st century damaged public trust in the accounting industry, necessitating reforms (Coates, 2007; Coffee, 2002). Due to ambiguous financial instruments and extreme risk-taking, the 2008 global financial crisis brought ethical considerations in accounting practices to light (Stiglitz, 2010). In response, regulatory and professional groups paid more attention to ethical rules. For example, the International Ethics Standards Board for Accountants (IESBA) updated its Code of Ethics for Professional Accountants in 2018 to stress the importance of honesty and fairness (Barrainkua & Espinosa-Pike, 2015).

In contemporary times, CSR and sustainability are becoming more important. This has revived interest in accounting's ethical foundations, which require a more interdependent world. The amalgamation of sustainability and CSR engendered novel reporting frameworks, namely the Global Reporting Initiative (GRI) and the International Integrated Reporting Council (IIRC) (Adams & Zutshi, 2004).

These frameworks emphasize the imperative of comprehensive reporting beyond financial performance and considering ESG factors (Berisha et al., 2022;

Elitaş & Üç, 2009; Uc & Shehu, 2017). New standards and guidelines were created in response to the growing call for ethics, such as the Sustainability Accounting Standards Board's (SASB) and the International Accounting Standards Board's (IASB) efforts to reveal ESG-related information.

2.1.1 Professional Codes of Conduct, Guidelines, and Ethical Behavior Among Accounting Professionals

Professional codes of conduct and ethical guidelines greatly impact accountants' rules, principles, and regulations, even though the field is dynamic and always changing (Mintz & Morris, 2022; Mussari et al., 2020). These codes clarify what accountants should do morally by focusing on honesty, objectivity, and discretion. They also strongly condemn dishonest behavior and situations where there are conflicting interests (Fisher & Lovell, 2009).

These codes, which evolved over centuries to include ethical duties to society and the common good, greatly impact accounting practices (Moore et al., 2006) by promoting transparency, accountability, public interest, and confidence (Mazzara et al., 2023; Tommasetti et al., 2021).

The proliferation of companies and the rise of accounting as a discipline in the 19th and 20th centuries led to ethical accounting protocols (Chatfield, 1977). During their formative years, codes of conduct were principally preoccupied with preserving the proficient norms of accounting experts (Parker, 1994).

Over time, these codes slowly expanded to include ethical issues, emphasizing accountants' duty to protect society's well-being (Previts & Merino, 1979). This change happened mostly because of financial wrongdoings that showed how important ethical behavior is for maintaining the integrity and credibility of accounting (Baker & Hayes, 2004).

Second-half 20th-century organizations realized the importance of ethics in determining the profession's character and maintaining public confidence, changing professional ethical standards (Duska & Duska, 2003). Because of this, today's ethical codes of trust protect truthfulness, fairness, privacy, and the duty of accountants to serve their clients and the community (Fisher & Lovell, 2009). These codes of conduct are a complex web of moral principles.

As ethical standards evolved, companies refined their regulatory systems to address moral transgressions (Fischer & Rosenzweig, 1995), ensure morality, and promote accountability. Additionally, an effort was made to incorporate ethical principles into accounting education and training to develop greater moral awareness and discernment among accounting professionals (Dellaportas, 2006).

To date, ethical codes of conduct function as guiding principles, steering accounting professionals through the intricate maze of ethical quandaries and predicaments they confront in their routine professional undertakings (Greenfield et al., 2008). These codes help practitioners make decisions in ethically ambiguous situations by providing a framework of precepts and ideals (Mintz & Morris, 2022).

Codes of conduct shape the ethical environment in organizations and regulate professional behavior (Greenfield et al., 2008). By feeding uprightness and moral rectitude, organizations can amplify their staff's attitude toward ethical mores and curtail the peril of deceitful conduct and misrepresentation. By clarifying what moral duties accountants have, these codes make people more aware of their responsibility for the effects of their actions, which discourages bad behavior and encourages good behavior (Fischer & Rosenzweig, 1995). The inculcation of ethical consciousness and comprehension among accounting professionals is an indispensable facet of implementing ethical protocols (Dellaportas, 2006).

These protocols raise ethical awareness in the accounting field, which gives professionals the power to make decisions in tough moral situations (Fischer & Rosenzweig, 1995; Mintz & Morris, 2022). The extent to which practitioners embrace ethical precepts is contingent upon several variables, from individual idiosyncrasies and collective organizational values to regulatory frameworks and education. Professionals' values impact ethical principles (Tsui, 1996); those with strong moral convictions and sound moral reasoning skills are more likely to act ethically, even in the face of outside influences (Douglas et al., 2001). On the contrary, feeble moral convictions or deficient reasoning abilities can potentially engender the manifestation of unethical conduct (Ponemon, 1992).

Cohen et al. (1998) say organizational culture also affects moral behavior. For example, if a company's culture puts profits ahead of morals, it may encourage employees to behave badly (Kaptein, 2008a; Schein, 2010).

The environment is another factor affecting ethical codes and guidelines (Shafer et al., 2001). According to Sikka (2015a), a strong regulatory framework with clear rules, strict enforcement, and violation penalties could encourage responsibility and deter professionals from breaking ethical standards. Lax or inconsistent ethical standards may allow professionals to break moral standards without consequence (Jackson et al., 2013).

Even the significance of accounting education in molding the mindset of professionals toward ethical codes and guidelines should not be underestimated (Dellaportas, 2006). Students can deeply understand morality and accounting practice through a comprehensive and multifaceted accounting education that also includes ethical considerations (Mintz & Morris, 2022). On the contrary, an educational curriculum that fails to incorporate ethical dimensions may render future practitioners unprepared to behave opportunely.

2.1.2 Ethical Implications of Decision-Making in Accounting, Financial Reporting, and Auditing

The convoluted nature of accounting decision-making mandates a comprehensive scrutiny of the ethical dimensions underlying this discipline's diverse facets. To thoroughly comprehend the ethical underpinnings that mold accounting practices, it is useful to contemplate the ethical ramifications intrinsic to accounting decision-making and the plausible outcomes of unethical practices for stake-holders and the broader society.

The accounting profession encapsulates various cognitive operations, each possessing its distinctive ethical facet (Jones, 1991). Ethical deliberations hold a pre-eminent position within the financial reporting domain, given that the authenticity of financial statements can have critical implications for stakeholders (Gray et al., 1996). In a parallel vein, the ethical conduct of auditors holds paramount importance in upholding the rectitude of the profession and cultivating reliance on financial data (Duska et al., 2018). These considerations explain why unscrupulous bookkeeping methodologies can affect stakeholders and broader society (Bampton & Cowton, 2013; Clikeman, 2009; Rezaee, 2005).

Ethical financial narration requires accurate and complete data to enable stakeholder decision-making based on truthful information. Manipulating or misrepresenting financial statements can have dire ramifications for stakeholders and the broader economy (Clikeman, 2009; Nobes, 2011).

Ethical issues arise when accountants manipulate financial data to satisfy management or improve the organization's image (Bazerman et al., 2002). The ethical dimension of financial reporting is intertwined with professional discretion because accountants must navigate the complexities of accounting and the uniqueness of each organization's reporting (Rajgopal, 1999). Impartial accounting principles and financial data representation are necessary for ethical financial reporting (Loeb, 1991).

The ethical requirements for financial reporting include disclosure transparency, which gives stakeholders complete information to make informed decisions (Eccles & Krzus, 2010). The ethical nature issue emerges in ascertaining the optimal degree of revelation, as companies are compelled to harmonize the necessity of transparency with safeguarding confidential data and the probable aftermaths of revealing delicate information (De George et al., 2016).

Because auditors must trust financial statements, auditing is meaningful and ethically complex. Internal auditing conflicts of interest can compromise ethical auditors' objectivity. The two ethical dilemmas auditors face are protecting confidential information and reporting fraud or illegal activity (Duska et al., 2018).

Simultaneously, auditors must show professional skepticism to find fraud or misrepresentation (DeAngelo, 1981). The endeavor toward skepticism may engender ethical issues when auditors are forced to restrict audit procedures or repress unfavorable discoveries (Nelson, 2009).

Another crucial aspect of the ethical auditing profession is stringent quality control, which ensures that relevant standards, ethics, and regulatory requirements carry out audit engagements (Francis & Yu, 2009). According to Knechel et al. (2013), cultivating an environment that promotes accountability and ensures the strict observance of quality control protocols can reduce the risks of unethical conduct while increasing confidence in accounting and auditing.

2.1.2.1 *Consequences of Unethical Accounting Practices on Stakeholders and Society*

Using ethically questionable accounting methodologies can have extensive ramifications for stakeholders, including investors, employees, creditors, regulators, customers, and suppliers. Individual and institutional investors use financial data to evaluate the interplay between investment perils and gains. If these data are compromised, investors may mistakenly evaluate a company's performance and prospects, risking substantial losses (Karpoff et al., 2008).

The integrity of fiscal declarations is paramount for creditors, encompassing banks, bondholders, and other financial establishments, as they employ them to evaluate a corporation's monetary stability and inclination toward insolvency. The act of distorting or manipulating fiscal information may inadvertently lead to the protraction of credit to individuals lacking merit or the exposure of oneself to superfluous hazards (Bushman & Smith, 2001).

Customers who trust their businesses' fiscal reliability and morality may experience resource flow delays, reduced product and service selection, or loss of access to essential goods and services due to unprincipled accounting practices (Hanson et al., 2016). Similarly, suppliers may encounter impediments in their associations with firms involved in unscrupulous accounting methodologies (Hanson et al., 2016).

Unscrupulous accounting methodologies yield significant ramifications for those with vested interests and give rise to extensive societal implications that reverberate throughout the economic, social, and political spheres. Employing ethically questionable accounting methodologies may engender market inefficiencies, misrepresent price signals, and misallocate resources (Healy & Palepu, 2003). Furthermore, the waning involvement of investors and the concomitant decrease in capital accumulation may hinder economic expansion and societal advancement.

The instantiation of ethically dubious accounting methodologies may also engender pernicious ramifications for collective cohesion and trust in institutions. Accounting scandals exemplify the transformative nature of public sentiment toward companies and the accounting discipline in general (Bazerman et al., 2002). Unemployment, social mobility, and social welfare provision erosion are all symptoms of this negative transformation (Jennings, 2014).

Public outcry often prompts legislators to correct unethical accounting practices. For example, the 2002 Sarbanes-Oxley Act was a typical legislative response to Enron and other bookkeeping scandals (Romano, 2005). However, although augmented regulation may restore confidence and foster transparency, it could also levy significant expenses on companies and impede ingenuity (Zingales, 2009). Politicizing accounting standards and regulatory oversight may also have unintended consequences because policymakers may bow to interest groups or short-term political pressures (Ramanna, 2008).

2.1.3 Corporate Governance and Ethical Accounting Practices

The balance between corporate governance mechanisms and accounting practitioners' ethical conduct holds a pre-eminent position in cultivating an environment of reliance, transparency, and accountability within organizations. According to Aguilera and Cuervo-Cazurra (2004), establishing corporate governance structures serves as the cornerstone for the ethical conduct of accounting practitioners.

By implementing sturdy governance frameworks, organizations can foster virtuous conduct and deter deceitful endeavors by encapsulating many elements, including board composition, coordination mechanisms, and internal control systems. These elements, in turn, serve as the fundamental pillars that underpin the promotion of ethical accounting practices (Beasley et al., 2000).

The myriad facets of the composition and configuration of a corporation's board of directors bear profound ramifications for the ethical conduct of accounting practitioners, encompassing the magnitude of the board, its heterogeneity, autonomy, and the existence of financial competencies. The size of the board holds sway over its efficacy in supervising the company's financial disclosures and ethical conduct.

Coles et al. (2008) found conflicting epistemological results on the ideal board size for ethical accounting. Larger boards may have more diverse expertise and experience but also drawbacks (Jensen, 1993; Yermack, 1996). Lipton and Lorsch (1992) suggest that small boards may be more agile and improve communication but lack diversity of skills and perspectives.

Diverse board members across genders, skills, and professional backgrounds can improve decision-making and accounting practice supervision (Adams & Ferreira, 2009; Carter et al., 2003). Erhardt et al. (2003) believe heterogeneous boards are more likely to challenge preconceived notions and inspire creativity, which promotes ethical accounting methods. Similarly, the inclusion of gender diversity within the board is also considered capable of engendering enhanced financial reporting caliber and a diminished probability of accounting malfeasance (Gul et al., 2011).

Regarding skills, including erudite members on the board can augment the caliber of financial disclosure and foster virtuous accounting methodologies. According to empirical accounting literature, corporate boards with finance experts can identify and prevent improprieties, reducing the risk of scandals (Abbott et al., 2004).

Risk assessment entails the discernment, scrutiny, and administration of potential hazards that could impinge upon the integrity and dependability of financial narrations. Through perpetual scrutiny of the likelihood of material misstatements and fraudulent activities, organizations can devise bespoke and efficacious internal mechanisms to alleviate such hazards (Simnett et al., 2009). A proactive stance toward risk assessment can serve as a measure against accounting malfeasance and foster ethical conduct among accounting practitioners by disclosing precise financial information (Knechel et al., 2013).

The efficacious dissemination of pertinent and timely financial information to all stakeholders, encompassing personnel, administration, and external organizations, is paramount. According to Francis and Armstrong (2003), organizations can effectively encourage ethical behavior and reduce the likelihood of accounting malfeasance by cultivating transparency and open communication. According to Cohen et al. (1998), companies with solid information and communication infrastructures exhibit higher financial reporting standards and ethical behavior.

Finally, organizational culture further shapes accounting practitioners' demeanor and ethical conduct. Cultivating a robust ethical culture engenders a context wherein virtuous conduct is incentivized while unethical behavior is dissuaded (Treviño et al., 1998). Empirical accounting research reveals that organizations that espouse a robust ethical ethos are inclined to manifest fewer occurrences of financial misrepresentation, deceit, and unscrupulous behavior (Douglas et al., 2001; Treviño et al., 2006).

2.1.4 Culture of Ethical Accountability

The accounting profession's credibility and community trust depend on ethical accountability among organizations and practitioners (Duska et al., 2018). Enacting clear rules, encouraging open communication and reporting, and providing targeted incentives for ethical behavior can achieve this goal.

The basis for ethical accountability is the careful creation of clear rules and protocols that outline the core values, principles, and benchmarks that should direct the behavior of people working within organizational structures (Mintz & Morris, 2022). These rules shape accounting professionals' ethical conduct and help them identify ethical issues (O'Leary, 2009). Defining clear rules involves four steps that improve the ethical framework: identifying fundamental ethical values and principles, turning them into functional guidelines, and assimilating and spreading them.

Establishing ethical policies and guidelines requires recognizing and expressing the accounting profession's core values and principles (Duska et al., 2018). These values and principles encompass integrity, objectivity, confidentiality, professionalism, and public interest. As Cohen et al. (1998) explained, the essence of ethical accounting practice is when these virtues appear together (Kaptein, 2008b).

Upon identifying the fundamental ethical values and principles, the subsequent course of action entails transmuting them into operational guidelines that provide pragmatic counsel on navigating through particular ethical quandaries and predicaments that may arise in the trajectory of accounting practice (Mintz & Morris, 2022). This may require methods and systems for ethical dilemmas, financial data disclosure, and compliance with relevant laws and norms.

Verschoor (1998) states that effective execution requires organizations to assimilate and spread ethical values and principles. Institutional accounting frameworks, methods, and techniques must match ethical paradigms (Greenberg, 1994). Since ethical principles and values are difficult to apply in complex situations, organizations must invest in training their employees (Simnett & Huggins, 2015).

Simnett and Huggins (2015) state that open communication channels and comprehensive reporting mechanisms in organizational frameworks are essential for ethical accountability. By encouraging ethical concerns and reporting misconduct, organizations can promote transparency. Organizations must use psychological safety, trust, and anonymous reporting mechanisms to achieve this goal.

Creating a psychologically safe and trustworthy organizational environment is the first condition for open communication and reporting (Edmondson, 1999). To avoid retaliation or negative outcomes, the workforce must feel confident when raising ethical concerns (Detert & Burris, 2007; Van Dyne et al., 2003).

By using digital platforms that allow anonymous reporting, companies can make it easier for employees to voice their ethical concerns without worrying about punishment (Miceli et al., 2008). These mechanisms must have strict confidentiality protocols and the organization's unwavering commitment to investigate and address all concerns, according to Callahan and Dworkin (1994).

Synchronizing incentives and rewards with ethical behavior strengthens the ethical accountability that organizations and individual practitioners bear (Alfawaz et al., 2010). By integrating ethical metrics into evaluating performances, decisions regarding promotions, and compensation structures, organizations can evince their dedication to ethical excellence and inspire their personnel to abide by the most elevated standards of ethical conduct (Treviño et al., 2000). Additionally, organizations can foster a sense of ethical accountability by enforcing consequences for unethical behavior and encouraging virtuous conduct (Luo & Bhattacharya, 2006).

Organizations must implement a comprehensive system of incentives to encourage ethical conduct and deter wrongdoing, including performance evaluation and reward recognition to promote virtue and duty. The design of appraisal and remuneration frameworks that incorporate ethical considerations is crucial to encouraging moral conduct and accountability (Treviño et al., 2014).

Organizations can lead employees to act ethically by integrating performance metrics and remuneration schemes (Alfawaz et al., 2010). Performance evaluations may need ethics codes, ethics-focused training, and ethical discernment (Fisher & Lovell, 2009).

Public commendation, awards, and distinctions assimilate ethical considerations into performance and remuneration systems, thereby fortifying the significance of ethical conduct within the organizational framework (Baucus et al., 2008). Organizations can cultivate a profound sense of self-esteem and commitment to moral principles within their cadre of employees by acknowledging and bestowing accolades upon those who surpass the mere fulfillment of their obligations (Meyer & Herscovitch, 2001).

2.1.4.1 Accounting Education, Professional Development, and Ethical Values

Integrating ethical values and principles into accounting is crucial to maintaining the credibility of this discipline. The pedagogical and professional initiatives aimed at fostering the growth of accounting practitioners are instrumental in feeding the ethical conduct of both individuals and organizations.

The integration of ethics into professional advancement initiatives comes from the consideration that accounting is fraught with numerous ethical pitfalls, which erode the general public's confidence and mandate collaborative endeavors to inculcate ethical principles among professionals (Bampton & Maclagan, 2005). The complexity of modern accounting methods has created unprecedented ethical dilemmas, requiring constant vigilance (Huss & Patterson, 1993).

Starting with appropriate academic curricula emphasizes the importance of professional development and ethical tutelage (Boon, 2011). Imbuing ethical principles into the accounting syllabus arises from the desire to foster practitioners who act ethically and preserve the profession's integrity (Dellaportas, 2006).

To include ethical values in accounting, teachers must develop new teaching methods that encourage students to do ethical and well-informed work. According to McPhail and Walters (2009), case-based learning gives students a unique chance to grapple with ethical issues and apply abstract paradigms to complex situations. Students can understand ethical dilemmas and question their beliefs by using Socratic dialectical inquiry and discerning thought.

Role-playing, simulations, and reflective experiments may also help students develop empathy, self-reflection, and ethical creativity. Accounting education should incorporate ethical principles and values throughout the curriculum (Greenfield et al., 2008). To achieve this aim, accounting programs should be outlined by employing an interdisciplinary outlook that acknowledges the inter-dependence of ethical deliberations with diverse subfields of the discipline (Cohen & Holder-Webb, 2006; Eynon et al., 1997).

To guarantee the efficacious amalgamation of ethics within the accounting syllabus, it is incumbent upon accounting pedagogues to utilize exacting appraisal techniques that gauge their pupils' ethical cognizance, aptitudes, and tendencies. According to Langenderfer and Rockness (1989), evaluation modalities that include tests, written assignments, oral presentations, and reflective appraisal instruments are suitable for capturing the essence of ethical proficiency. The findings of evaluations and the constantly evolving ethical dilemmas facing the accounting industry should guide the never-ending pursuit of improvement (Bean & Bernardi, 2007).

The efficacious formulation and execution of ethical education necessitate a discerning comprehension of the intended cognitive achievements, didactic methodologies, and situational variables that impact ethical maturation (Glass & Bonnici, 1997). Pedagogy should promote ethical values by emphasizing learner self-governance, practical experience, and professional relevance (Knowles, 1984).

Combining case studies, virtual reality exercises, and collaborative discussions is necessary to tailor ethical education programs to future accounting pro-fessionals' needs (Sweeney & Costello, 2009). Cultivating ethical principles should be steady, with ad hoc assessments and modifications to guarantee unceasing refinement (Duska et al., 2018).

Furthermore, harmonious cooperation between accounting educators, practi-tioners, and professional accounting bodies is essential for effective professional development programs and ethical education. To achieve this aim, the active involvement of various organizations, which can provide comprehensive direc-tives, support accreditation, and extend their support to sustain the perpetuity of professional education initiatives, can facilitate the expansion and execution of ethical training programs (Dellaportas, 2006). In this regard, the AICPA and the International Federation of Accountants (IFAC) are paramount in advancing standards, propagating methodologies, and furnishing ethical education resources (McPhail & Walters, 2009).

According to Sikka (2015b), the onus of cultivating and promulgating the ethical principles that regulate accounting practitioners' behavior predominantly rests upon professional accounting bodies. The AICPA Code of Professional Conduct and the IFAC Code of Ethics for Professional Accountants circumscribe some important ethical tenets and imperatives, providing a framework for contemplating ethical matters and establishing accountability (Cohen et al., 1998). As Everett et al. (2006) posited, accounting institutions are responsible for safeguarding the bond of public trust while simultaneously discerning arbiters of ethical issues through codifying norms.

In addition to their conventional role, professional accounting bodies function as the representatives of the accounting profession, espousing the significance of ethical accountability and fostering rectitude within the profession (Dellaportas, 2006). Using their scholarly publications and outreach endeavors, these institutions promulgate erudition and exemplars of excellence, nurturing a dialectic on ethical quandaries and instilling a dedication to elevated ethical benchmarks amidst the accounting profession (McPhail & Walters, 2009). Furthermore, it is noteworthy that professional accounting organizations collaborate with regulatory bodies, policymakers, and other stakeholders to promote the profession's ethical tenets and guarantee that accounting methodologies meet societal expectations (Hiltebeitel & Jones, 1992).

2.2 The Power of Transparency in Financial Reporting, Auditing, and Accountability

Transparency, a concept frequently invoked in accounting discourse, constitutes a fundamental pillar of the profession, serving as a bedrock for its credibility and fostering society's trust in its practitioners.

The implications of transparency in the accounting industry go beyond simply providing accurate and reliable financial data because the ethical foundations on which we build all our societal structures promote accountability, trust, and credibility. Beyond impartial and precise financial record evaluation, these values are essential to a just and equitable society.

Comprehending the power of transparency within the accounting domain necessitates thorough scrutiny of its various embodiments in financial reporting, auditing, and accountability. Financial reporting transparency relies on an organization's economic reality and financial data's intelligibility, promptness, and confirmability (Barth & Schipper, 2008). Transparent financial reporting promotes informed decision-making and resource allocation, which helps capital markets and the economy run smoothly (Nobes & Parker, 2008).

Transparent financial reporting must dutifully conform to the following qualitative attributes: relevance, faithful representation, comparability, verifiability, timeliness, and understandability (Penman, 2007). In tandem with the obligatory revelations mandated by accounting norms and edicts, organizations frequently partake in discretionary disclosures to increase the transparency of their narrations (Healy & Palepu, 2001).

Voluntarily disclosing information, including nonfinancial data, can provide meaningful insight into an organization's strategic orientation, hazard disposition, and competitive environment (Botosan & Plumlee, 2002). Voluntary disclosure helps an organization present a more complete performance picture. This helps stakeholders understand fundamental economic truths and make wise decisions (Leuz & Wysocki, 2016).

In auditing, transparency includes elucidating methodologies, disseminating findings, and enforcing quality control measures (Simnett et al., 2009). Through strict transparency, auditing strengthens stakeholders' trust in financial data and institutions of accountability.

The focal point of transparent auditing stands in the auditor's autonomy, which encompasses the moral conduct of the practitioner in executing their professional obligations (DeFond & Zhang, 2014). Preserving the audit process's credibility and dependability hinges on the importance of auditor independence. This protects the auditor's judgment from conflicts of interest (Lennox, 2005).

The committees entrusted with the duty of conducting audits assume a paramount function in pursuing transparency, entrusted with multifarious obligations encompassing the designation and engagement of auditors, scrutinizing audit schemes and discoveries, and assessing the auditors' efficiency and impartiality (DeZoort et al., 2002). Under their assiduous supervision, audit committees make a valuable contribution toward augmenting audit transparency, thereby fortifying stakeholder trust in the uprightness and excellence of the audit mechanism (Abbott et al., 2004).

Transparency also assumes a paramount position in accountability, encapsulating the ethical imperatives that steer the accounting profession. By providing transparent and intelligible explanations of an organization's financial undertakings, transparency in accountability begets reliance and authenticity among stakeholders while advancing the tenets of morality and credibility.

Transparency is a manifestation of accountability. Comprehensive disclosure of financial performance indicators, disclosure of possible conflicting interests, promotion of truthfulness, trust, and collective responsibility among involved parties, and ethical behavior and equitable resource distribution are all part of it. These various aspects of transparency within accountability are crucial for cultivating a virtuous and equitable organizational environment. It enables stakeholders to access relevant and accurate data and serves as a conduit for accountability (Roberts & Bobek, 2004). This gives stakeholders the power to hold organizational agents accountable for their conduct.

2.3 Lack of Trust and Credibility in the Accounting Profession

The profession of accounting, formerly upheld as a stronghold of trust, has of late borne witness to an alarming corrosion of its credibility. This issue can depend on several causes, encompassing corporate malfeasance, deceptive financial reports, and unscrupulous behaviors (Sikka, 2015b).

Corporate malfeasance highlights the risk of the inadequacy of accounting and auditing practices in detecting and preventing financial impropriety and the threat of professional collaboration in fraudulent companies (Coffee, 2002). This risk engenders a sense of skepticism regarding the accounting profession's aptitude to safeguard stakeholders' interests, thereby eroding the foundation upon which the profession is constructed (Nobes & Parker, 2008).

Cases of compromised objectivity, illicit remuneration, and exploitation of privileged information significantly erased stakeholder confidence (Amat et al., 1999; Clikeman, 2009; Duska et al., 2018). Negative reputation impacts extend beyond the profession, hindering its ability to fulfill its stakeholder obligations (Sikka, 2015a; Svanberg & Öhman, 2013).

Several scandals engendered pervasive shades over the profession, prompting apprehensions regarding the effectiveness of existing regulatory paradigms and the ethical bearings that steer the conduct of practitioners (Humphrey et al., 2009; Nobes & Parker, 2008). Unethical accounting practices violate the discipline's transparency, objectivity, and integrity principles, undermining society's trust in the profession's financial data (Clikeman, 2009).

In light of these apprehensions, institutions implemented modifications to augment supervision and foster heightened accountability (Carson et al., 2013; Sikka, 2015b). The regulatory endeavors were directed toward restoring trust, increasing responsibility, and propagating transparency within the profession (Carson et al., 2013). The creation and adoption of International Financial Reporting Standards (IFRS) was the most significant regulatory response to promote financial reporting transparency and comparability worldwide (Daske et al., 2008; Nobes & Parker, 2008).

Chapter 3

Convergence of Artificial Intelligence and Sustainable Innovation Reporting

3.1 Artificial Intelligence (AI) in Accounting Research

In this fast-changing technology world, AI impacts many human activities (Baldwin et al., 2006; Damerji & Salimi, 2021). The accounting field, which has long relied on conventional methods, also underwent significant changes as AI was developed and implemented. AI-based accounting apps vary in interesting and important ways (Fedyk et al., 2022; Issa et al., 2016).

For example, machine learning (ML), an important constituent of AI, exhibited high potential in scrutinizing financial statements. Vasarhelyi et al. (2015) state that building complex frameworks that show how economic variables are connected and reveal patterns beyond human understanding makes it easier.

Similarly, natural language processing (NLP) engenders a profound transformation in textual data analysis within the accounting domain. This change simplifies extracting useful information from large amounts of unstructured text data like financial reports and corporate disclosures (Li et al., 2016).

AI-powered algorithms improve fraud detection accuracy and speed, ushering in a new forensic accounting era. The mutually beneficial relationship between AI and the field of financial investigation is set to change how we understand and fight fraud completely. Nowadays, AI feeds the cultivation of novel models, techniques, and frameworks that expand the boundaries of accounting innovation. These frameworks use AI to pull actionable insights from large datasets faster than traditional accounting methods (Bonsón et al., 2015).

AI makes studying complex, nonlinear financial variable relationships and forecasting models that account for economic, social, and environmental factors easier. Our understanding of accounting phenomena improved, making it easier to contribute to managerial and policy discussions (Calo, 2017).

AI and accounting have created new paradigms for understanding real-life details. Deep learning and other AI-powered methods have created frameworks to determine how financial parameters relate. Consequently, this increased the prognostic precision of accounting models (Vasarhelyi et al., 2015).

Sustainable Innovation Reporting and Emerging Technologies, 29–48
Copyright © 2024 Gennaro Maione
Published under exclusive licence by Emerald Publishing Limited
doi:10.1108/978-1-83797-739-020241003

AI even reshaped the very fabric of data analysis within accounting research. It has produced innovative statistical methods and techniques. The field has entered intellectually uncharted territory. Accounting scholars can now find hidden patterns and connections in large datasets thanks to the development of AI-driven data mining methods (Bonsón et al., 2015). This makes getting deep insights and producing solid, empirically based conclusions easier.

AI has also made data sources and types blend well. Combining structured financial data and unstructured textual data led to cutting-edge data visualization techniques, making it easier for people with specialized and general knowledge to understand accounting connections (Pries & Dunnigan, 2015). Combining data sources led to cutting-edge data visualization techniques, making accounting connections easier for specialists and nonspecialists (Pries & Dunnigan, 2015). This integration allows a more all-encompassing comprehension of the accounting phenomenon (Li et al., 2016).

3.1.1 AI and Its Accounting Applications

One of the many uses of AI in accounting is to look at financial statements using ML techniques. Other uses include reading and analyzing text data using NLP techniques, automating some accounting tasks with robotic process automation (RPA), and finding fraud using AI. According to Han et al. (2023), ML is now used to look more closely at financial statements. Using supervised, unsupervised, deep, and ensemble learning paradigms and several techniques, such as sentiment analysis, topic modeling, and RPA, has led to new ways of doing things and insights.

Supervised learning uses annotated data to teach AI algorithms using linear regressions. Linear, logistic, and support vector regressions are used in financial analysis to figure out how complex economic variables are related. This lets analysts accurately predict sales, earnings, and stock prices. Many regression models exist, each with its purpose. Multiple linear regression seeks complex relationships between multiple predictors and a continuous outcome. Logistic regression examines binary outcomes and the complex relationship between predictors and event probability. The vector regression model uses vectors to navigate the complex terrain of continuous outcomes and predict optimally.

Unsupervised learning finds changes in known patterns for AI-driven anomaly detection, including fraud (Hodge & Austin, 2004). Similarity-based clustering algorithms like k-means and DBSCAN group financial transactions in computational analysis. This helps identify anomalies that may be fraudulent (Sun, 2019).

Deep learning, an ML form that uses multilayered artificial neural networks, is another helpful tool for analyzing financial statements. Deep learning models like convolutional neural networks work with grid-like data. They make finding patterns and extracting features from economic variable-time series data easier. A popular deep learning model is recurrent neural networks, which handle sequential data well. They can simulate financial ratios and earnings changes (Sezer & Ozbayoglu, 2018).

Ensemble learning combines different models, leading to better and higher performance in financial statement analysis, where its many benefits become clear. Using techniques like bagging, boosting, and stacking to create strong and useful models that exploit how well different ML algorithms work together (Polikar, 2006). These models can predict bankruptcy, credit risks, and business revenue by analyzing financial statements. This is possible by removing the limitations and predispositions that come with solitary ML methodologies (Kumar & Ravi, 2007).

Sentiment analysis allows for discerning the emotional value inherent in textual data. Its application has proven helpful when scrutinizing corporate disclosures, facilitating a deeper understanding of the nuances embedded within corporate decision-making and strategy (Li et al., 2016). Sentiment analysis also examines how a company's disclosure tone affects investor sentiment and decision-making. This helps understand financial markets (Tetlock, 2007).

The practice of topic modeling triggered a paradigm shift in financial document analysis. By scrutinizing textual data, including annual reports, analyst commentaries, and regulatory filings, this method allows for discerning and extracting essential themes. For instance, the Latent Dirichlet Allocation (LDA) algorithm is useful in topic modeling because it finds the hidden thematic framework in financial texts. This helps researchers understand the main issues that affect how investors behave and make decisions (Blei et al., 2003; Loughran & McDonald, 2016). Moreover, dynamic topic models are frequently used to capture the temporal evolution of topics. Specifically, these models let you track the appearance and disappearance of financial themes over time, giving you a full longitudinal view of how accounting discourse is always changing (Blei & Lafferty, 2006).

RPA, which automates repetitive, standard tasks, is changing accounting operations in accounts payable and receivable, payroll, audit and compliance, and more. RPA for accounts payable and receivable automates invoice processing, payments, and account reconciliation. This eliminates manual data entry, reducing the risk of human error. It also speeds up these processes, improving their efficiency. It also improves supplier relations and financial documentation (Cooper et al., 2019).

RPA payroll ensures accurate and timely payments by tracking employees' hours and attendance, calculating their pay, and keeping the company within budget. This reduces accounting professionals' workloads, reduces errors, and speeds up and improves wage payments (Davenport & Ronanki, 2018). By automating data extraction, sampling, and testing, RPA improved auditing and compliance. RPA streamlines the audit process, letting auditors focus on critical areas. Companies can monitor their internal controls continuously and detect and fix hidden control issues and compliance gaps before they occur (Appelbaum et al., 2017).

3.1.2 AI and the Development of New Accounting Models

AI in accounting has ushered in a new era of methodological progress, where research and the profession are attempting to capitalize on expanding technological capabilities. The most critical advances are valuation paradigms and risk assessment (Kokina & Davenport, 2017; Leoni et al., 2021).

Despite their widespread use, conventional valuation paradigms draw criticism for their reliance on historical data and subjective assumptions. When AI algorithms came along, they made traditional accounting valuation methods like discounted cash flow and residual income models very different.

With AI, new evaluation methods have emerged. These predict financial flows, discount rates, and valuation factors using ML and deep learning algorithms (Kokina & Davenport, 2017). Combining ML models like neural networks and regression trees makes financial forecasting more accurate and valuable (Penman, 2013).

In financial forecasting, financial statements, and market data analysis, AI-powered models look for complex patterns and correlations in huge amounts of structured and unstructured data (Brynjolfsson & McAfee, 2017). Accounting professionals can use complex models for sentiment, network, and anomaly detection in large datasets (Vasarhelyi et al., 2015). AI helps improve risk assessment models by analyzing massive amounts of data and finding complex patterns and connections that may indicate financial trouble (Baryannis et al., 2019).

The AI-based mechanisms can identify complex patterns, trends, and anomalies in financial data. The AI-based mechanisms can discern intricate patterns, discernible trends, and deviant occurrences within financial information.

The data from these systems can also improve managers' risk reduction, decision-making, and regulatory compliance. AI-based financial monitoring can combine financial statements and transaction records with news articles and social media posts. These sources enrich an organization's financial performance and risk profile (Giudici, 2018).

3.2 The Transformative Power of AI in Sustainable Innovation Reporting

While sustainability reporting is becoming an important part of corporate responsibility, AI is radically changing data collection and analysis techniques, metrics, reporting, and frameworks (Maione & Leoni, 2021; Zhang, Zhu, et al., 2023).

The vast amount of sustainability data and its complexity require highly refined AI algorithms to navigate it. The complex algorithms, which combine ML and NLP, simplify data acquisition and analysis from many sources. These sources cover various domains, from corporate reports and websites to social media and satellite imagery (Fisher et al., 2016).

Implementing AI in sustainability metrics and indicators has had a profound transformative effect. ML algorithms unveil an extraordinary capacity to discern intricate patterns and interconnections among sustainability indicators.

Through this remarkable cognitive prowess, companies are bestowed with an enhanced comprehension of the underlying forces that shape their sustainability performance. AI-powered analytics can also predict the effects of upcoming sustainability risks and opportunities, allowing companies to adapt their plans to a world that is always changing (Kumar & Ravi, 2007).

The advent of AI has undoubtedly assumed a paramount role in the progressive evolution of sustainable reporting frameworks and standards. Due to the growing interest in sustainability, AI-driven tools can combine different reporting frameworks and standards to create a more harmonious convergence. These instruments make it easier to compare and set standards for sustainable performance, which speeds up the search for overall sustainability.

Moreover, the advent of AI fosters the progression of ever more dynamic and receptive systems for reporting. These conceptual frameworks can naturally change to meet the needs of different stakeholders and our growing knowledge of sustainability issues, thanks to a two-way process (Meske et al., 2022).

The advent of AI has also profoundly influenced stakeholder engagement within sustainability reporting. Companies can find out how their stakeholders feel and what they want regarding sustainability issues by using AI-powered sentiment analysis and NLP. This discernment bestows organizations with the ability to tailor their sustainability reports and communications more coherently.

AI makes stakeholder engagement even more effective by figuring out and prioritizing their most important concerns. This enables organizations to formulate strategies that adequately tackle these concerns and foster a sense of trust and collaboration among the stakeholders (Güngör, 2020).

3.2.1 AI-Enabled Data Collection and Processing in Sustainability Reporting

Data collection and processing in sustainability reporting are multifaceted problems, entailing many intricacies about their voluminous nature, diverse array, and authenticity. Ensuring accurate and quick data collection and integration from many sources requires creative solutions (Bienvenido-Huertas et al., 2020).

AI-driven methods like ML and NLP can extract knowledge from corporate reports, digital domains, and satellite imagery. These advanced methods make it faster to look at unstructured data, which lets companies include qualitative data like stakeholders' thoughts and feelings in their sustainability reports (Moodaley & Telukdarie, 2023). From now on, methods for collecting and processing data based on AI could help understand sustainability performance and the basic factors that affect it more completely.

Yet another salient facet of AI's contribution to data collection and processing in sustainability reporting is its aptitude for predictive analytics. Organizations can scrutinize archival data through ML algorithms, discerning patterns and trends. This knowledge then allows organizations to predict what will happen regarding sustainability (Calabrese et al., 2023) and to see what risks and opportunities might arise. This lets them make decisions and take action to deal with growing sustainability issues.

Through the implementation of automated mechanisms for data collection and processing, AI can substantially diminish the propensity for human fallibility. This engenders sustainability reports imbued with heightened precision and dependability. More than that, AI's ability to accurately and efficiently take in huge amounts of information could speed up sending out reports. This expeditiousness enables organizations to address stakeholders' concerns and promptly fulfill regulatory obligations (Bonsón et al., 2021).

AI data collection and processing can also simplify sustainability indicator combinations, resulting in a more comprehensive sustainability performance assessment. AI creates more durable and useful sustainability methods, which inspire organizational responsibility and openness (Duan et al., 2019).

3.2.2 AI, Sustainability Metrics, and Indicators

The exigencies of sustainable development necessitate organizations to devise innovative methodologies for quantifying and divulging their sustainability efforts, a matter of escalating pertinence within the contemporary business environment. AI is a powerful helper in this situation that could cause a paradigm shift in developing new sustainability metrics and indicators for full reporting.

AI technologies are catalysts for unearthing hitherto uncharted realms of sustainability performance, propelling the accounting domain forward. By scrutinizing copious amounts of organized and unorganized data, AI algorithms can discern intricate patterns, correlations, and causal connections (Bebbington & Unerman, 2018). AI tools could lead to the creation of more complex and refined measures of sustainability that can include all the different aspects of sustainable success. Consequently, such a development fosters a comprehensive and unified methodology for disseminating sustainability information (Nishant et al., 2020).

AI can also make sustainability metrics more honest, reliable, and useful. Detailed historical data analysis using ML algorithms is promising. This will help organizations confirm and improve their sustainability metrics with real-world evidence. AI-driven methods, sentiment analysis, and semantic analysis significantly impact knowledge extraction (Chui et al., 2018).

The perspicuity, accuracy, and dependability of organizations' information are critical components of sustainable innovation reporting. Using metrics that AI drives can make sustainability reporting clearer by making it easier to validate and check data more thoroughly. ML algorithms can discern aberrations, deviances, and contradictions within sustainability data. This, in turn, empowers organizations to redress plausible fallacies and distortions that may have permeated their sustainability reports. AI could make standardizing and comparing sustainability metrics and indicators easier across companies and industries, increasing openness and transparency (Di Vaio et al., 2020).

Including nonmonetary data in sustainability reporting effectively is another important way AI is helping to create new sustainability metrics. Traditional financial accounting and reporting methods often have trouble advantageously integrating nonfinancial information. This separates a company's finances from nonfinancials. By harnessing its capabilities, organizations can effectively navigate the labyrinth of nonfinancial information, environmental data, and social data in tandem with financial data. This harmonious fusion yields sustainability metrics that are both comprehensive and seamlessly integrated (Bebbington & Unerman, 2018).

AI-driven metrics have a lot of potential to expand the scope of sustainability reporting by including aspects that have not been looked at or given enough attention. These include how ESG factors create long-term value and reduce risks (Baryannis et al., 2018). AI can also favor heightened uniformity and comparability within sustainability reporting. This is achieved by cultivating a shared lexicon of sustainability metrics and indicators that permeate diverse organizations and industries (Bienvenido-Huertas et al., 2020).

3.2.3 AI and Stakeholder Engagement in Sustainability Reporting

AI in sustainability reporting has created many opportunities for stakeholder engagement, which is crucial to a strong reporting framework (Adams & McNicholas, 2007). Organizations can share and receive information from their many stakeholders more easily and quickly thanks to AI (Brown et al., 2009).

Companies can simplify complex sustainability data for stakeholders using AI-powered data visualization tools. Stakeholders can assess the organization's sustainability and innovation performance. AI-powered data visualization tools can help find and share sustainability data trends, patterns, and connections. This fosters smart, fact-based decision-making among all parties (Hockerts & Moir, 2004).

Another important way that AI can help increase stakeholder engagement is by creating more thorough and collaborative reporting methods. These methods promote societal awareness, individual freedom, and long-lasting creativity (Adams & McNicholas, 2007). Organizations can involve stakeholders using AI-powered platforms like virtual forums, knowledge repositories, and collaborative tools. Such platforms let them share their ideas, experiences, and points of view in reporting (Freeman et al., 2010).

AI helps organizations see and respond to stakeholder feedback and expectations. This helps them adapt and move forward with changing sustainability challenges. AI-powered sentiment analysis and social listening can reveal stakeholders' thoughts, feelings, and expectations (Eccles et al., 2014).

AI can also enable heightened precision and effectiveness in communication strategies. Meeting stakeholders' different informational needs and personal preferences creates a customized and user-centered system for sharing sustainability reports (Klettner et al., 2014). Organizations can ensure that their sustainability reports and communications align with the interests, values, and priorities of a wide range of stakeholders by using AI-driven segmentation and personalization techniques. These techniques also help build trust and transparency. This effort makes sustainable innovation reporting more relevant, effective, and resonant (Velte & Stawinoga, 2017).

AI can boost trust and transparency by improving sustainability data and disclosure accuracy, dependability, and verifiability. AI-driven data validation and error detection can help companies find and fix sustainability data discrepancies. Thus, their sustainability reports are more credible (Bhimani & Langfield-Smith, 2007).

AI-driven analytics and ML help companies understand their sustainability efforts' deep complexities. This gives stakeholders a more detailed, comprehensive, and situational understanding of their sustainability prowess and progress, which boosts their trust and confidence in their ability to create lasting sustainable value (Hahn & Kühnen, 2013).

AI can also improve sustainability report accessibility, navigability, and usability. AI-driven NLP can help companies condense their sustainability reports into clearer, logically connected narratives. This creates a positive environment for stakeholder involvement and understanding, which deepens engagement and understanding. AI-powered search and recommendation engines can help stakeholders find and use sustainability data. This improves reporting transparency and user-centricity (Han et al., 2023).

Organizations can see and deal with new patterns, risks, and chances in sustainability by using AI-driven predictive analytics and real-time data surveillance (Bonsón & Bednárová, 2022). Finally, AI can improve trust and openness by making it easier for quick, flexible, and open reporting methods that accurately reflect how sustainability problems and opportunities are always changing.

3.3 Professional Bodies and Regulators and Ethical AI-Driven Accounting Practices

How clear, complete, and convincing the moral imperatives are and how well accounting professionals understand and follow them will determine how well these rules and guidelines encourage ethical behavior among AI professionals (Davenport & Harris, 2005). Professional groups must work hard to develop ethical standards and guidelines based on a deep understanding of AI's moral issues.

To navigate the shifting ethical landscape of AI-augmented accounting, professional bodies should also keep the conversation going, encourage peaceful collaboration, and make it simpler for accountants, regulators, policymakers, and other stakeholders to share their knowledge.

The regulatory and professional bodies work together to use AI in accounting ethically. They do this by closely monitoring and enforcing the rules. The regulatory authorities create and enforce laws, rules, and guidelines governing AI in accounting. Regulators punish those who violate ethical standards. Additionally, they are tasked with diligently monitoring regulatory compliance to maintain society's moral order (Appelbaum et al., 2017).

AI algorithms' enigmatic nature makes identifying and punishing ethical transgressions difficult, which is just one of the challenges of regulating AI-driven accounting practices. The lack of a global AI regulatory structure is a concern.

This absence creates disparities across jurisdictions and raises ethical questions about AI-driven accounting. AI development and spread may be too fast for regulators to keep up with ethical risks and vulnerabilities. This requires regulators to develop more flexible, fast, and foresighted methods (Appelbaum et al., 2017).

3.3.1 Regulatory Oversight and Enforcement in AI-Driven Accounting

As accounting uses more AI, regulators must remember their main role in overseeing and enforcing ethical standards. Regulators face many ethical issues when traditional accounting methods meet new technology (Chui et al., 2016).

As part of their job, regulators are responsible for developing and spreading general rules about using AI ethically in accounting practices. Set up frameworks and detailed protocols and explain the basics of bringing AI technologies into accounting (Appelbaum et al., 2017). Regulatory bodies tell professionals how to deal with the tricky ethical issues and possible problems that might come up by outlining the moral duties and requirements of using AI in accounting (Appelbaum et al., 2017).

Regulators help accounting professionals share knowledge and use the best methods. This goal can be achieved by setting up workshops, seminars, and other learning opportunities to help people understand AI-driven accounting ethical issues. Collective efforts raise ethics and responsibility, making it ideal for following rules and guidelines (Srinivasan & González, 2022).

Regulatory bodies must be vigilant to ensure ethical standards and AI principles are followed. To ensure that accounting professionals and organizations follow the rules and guidelines, they can conduct audits, investigations, and inspections. Regulators' penalties, fines, and other corrective actions can emphasize the value of ethical conduct and accountability in AI accounting (Susskind & Susskind, 2015).

Integral to reporting standards is ethical AI in accounting. Regulatory bodies must develop, improve, and regularly update reporting systems to make it easier to demonstrate how AI technologies have changed financial statements and other disclosures (Gray et al., 2014). For people to trust each other and the system, regulators must give AI-driven accounting practices more credibility and dependability (Susskind & Susskind, 2015).

Regulations struggle with AI's rapid technological advancements. New AI-based technologies require regulators to stay abreast of them to tailor guidelines, standards, and enforcement (Brynjolfsson & McAfee, 2014). Thus, harmonization with scholars, professionals, and policymakers is essential to understanding AI developments and their ethical implications.

AI algorithms often appear as "black boxes," making their cognitive processes opaque. Regulators must understand these algorithms to assess their ethical behavior and identify hidden biases. Standardized methods for examining AI-based accounting systems could solve this problem, but research and development will be expensive (Buiten, 2019).

Multiple jurisdictions using AI-driven accounting methods make regulators' monitoring harder. Today's globalized companies use AI-based accounting methods in multiple jurisdictions, each with its own rules and morals. Different regulators from different countries must work together to supervise AI-driven accounting practices consistently and effectively (Gray et al., 2014).

3.4 Case Study: Unilever and AI-Driven Sustainable Innovation Reporting

Unilever is a global company founded in 1929 from the merger of two companies, Lever Brothers in England and Margarine Unie in the Netherlands. Since 1930, the organization has worked to expand its reach into diverse markets. The markets include personal care, beauty and well-being, home care, nutrition, and ice cream. The company has over 400 recognized brands with an appeal that spans 190 countries. AI in accounting and ethical, sustainable innovation reporting are two examples of the company's commitment to cutting-edge technologies and methods that have helped it succeed.

Unilever, which earned over 60 billion euros in 2022 and had over 127,000 employees, shows how important and useful AI can be for reporting sustainable innovation. Unilever pioneered sustainable innovation reporting in the 1990s by establishing one of the consumer goods industry's first environmental management systems. The company also consistently ranks high in the Dow Jones Sustainability Index and Corporate Knights.

Unilever advocates balancing economic growth with social and environmental protection. Sustainability has driven the company to use cutting-edge technologies like AI to address sustainable innovation reporting challenges and opportunities.

A key junction point in Unilever's journey toward sustainability materialized in 2010, when the Unilever Sustainable Living Plan (USLP) was drafted, heralding a profound shift in the company's ethics. The company had a strong ecological and positive social impact from then on.

The USLP set goals like reducing greenhouse gas emissions, water stewardship, and social inclusivity (Lawrence et al., 2018). With several initiatives and programs focused on climate change, nature conservation, the circular economy, and improving people's welfare and health, the company made remarkable progress in achieving USLP goals.

3.4.1 Research Design

An in-depth study of secondary data was carried out to look closely at how AI is used in Unilever's organization to report on sustainable innovation. The purpose was to delve into the depths of Unilever's dedication to sustainability, scrutinize its reporting practices, and ponder AI's influence on its operations.

Several annual sustainability reports were analyzed. Furthermore, in-depth scrutiny was conducted on the financial statements. This facilitated a better comprehension of the financial ramifications of Unilever's sustainability endeavors and the influence of AI in propelling these efforts. Several corporate strategy documents were also examined, encompassing mission statements, vision documents, strategic action plans, press conferences, and presentations. Table 1 schematizes the records analyzed for this case study.

The array of document types provided elucidations regarding Unilever's modus operandi in sustainability and the imprint of AI on its reporting methodologies. The collected data were subsequently examined by employing a thematic analysis. It is a method aimed at discerning, scrutinizing, and elucidating recurring patterns (themes) inherent within the qualitative data (Braun & Clarke, 2006). Thematic analysis has six separate steps: getting to know the data; producing a set of codes to capture the essence of the data; finding the themes that run through the data; studying and refining these themes to make sure they make

Table 1. Dataset of the Case Study Unilever.

Year	Document Type	Number of Documents	Specifics
2012–2022	Annual sustainability report	11	Commitment to sustainability, focus on sustainable practices and reporting, introduction and expansion of AI in operations (Unilever, 2012, 2013, 2014, 2015, 2016, 2017, 2018, 2019, 2020, 2021, 2022)
2013–2022	Financial statement	10	Insights into financial implications of sustainability initiatives, evolution of AI's role in these initiatives (Unilever, 2013, 2014, 2015, 2016, 2017, 2018, 2019, 2020, 2021, 2022)
Several years	Corporate strategy document	8	Mission statements, vision documents, and strategic action plans highlighting company's focus on sustainability and AI (Unilever, 2016, 2017, 2018, 2019, 2020, 2021)
Several years	Press conferences and presentation	7	Detailed insights from company's executives on sustainability strategies and the use of AI in sustainability reporting (Unilever, 2023)

the most sense; giving these themes labels to capture their essence; and finally, writing a full report that summarizes the results of the analysis.

The encoding process was carried out using an open-coding methodology. This necessitated the allocation of labels to portions of textual material pertinent to scholarly aims. Twelve codes have been created to represent how AI can be used in Unilever's sustainability reporting, including both the good things about it and the problems it can cause. Table 2 lists these codes, classified into three domains: application, benefits, and challenges.

Subsequently, the codes were arranged according to their intrinsic resemblances and interconnections. The process ended with discovering five main themes (shown in Table 3) that gave the collected data a conceptual framework for understanding. The themes identified functioned as the fundamental underpinnings for the exposition and contemplation of empirical findings.

3.4.2 Findings and Discussion

Unilever's dedication to integrating AI within its accounting and sustainability reporting practices testifies to its visionary mindset and unyielding pursuit of perpetual refinement. The AI applications that have been very important in changing Unilever's accounting and sustainability reporting include automating and processing data, improving reporting and disclosure methods, enhancing metrics and indicators, and making communication with stakeholders easier.

Unilever is improving its accounting and sustainability reporting by measuring and reporting performance, promoting sustainable development, and collecting

Table 2. Codes.

Area	Code
Application of AI in sustainable reporting practices	• AI algorithms • Machine learning models • Data analysis • Automation
Benefits of AI-based tools	• Efficiency improvement • Predictive analytics • Decision-making support • Resource optimization
Challenges associated with AI implementation	• Data privacy • Ethical considerations • Transparency • Implementation complexity

Table 3. Themes.

Theme	Description
Algorithms and models	This theme focuses on utilizing advanced AI algorithms and models in Unilever's sustainable innovation reporting. It explores how AI algorithms and models are applied to analyze and interpret sustainability data for improved insights and decision-making
Environmental impact	This theme delves into Unilever's efforts to assess and mitigate its environmental impact. It explores the company's strategies, practices, and initiatives to reduce carbon emissions, conserve natural resources, minimize waste generation, and promote sustainable supply chains
Reporting standards	This theme focuses on the reporting standards and frameworks employed by Unilever in its sustainability reporting. It examines the transparency, accuracy, and completeness of Unilever's sustainability disclosures, including the scope of reported data, key performance indicators (KPIs), and targets for measuring progress toward sustainability goals
Social responsibility	This theme explores Unilever's commitment to social responsibility and its initiatives to impact communities and society positively. It examines the company's stakeholder engagement to address social issues and promote sustainable development
Data privacy and ethics	This theme focuses on data privacy, security, and ethics in implementing AI technologies at Unilever. It examines the measures taken to protect personal and sensitive data, ensure compliance with data protection regulations, and safeguard stakeholders' privacy. It also assesses the company's approach to responsible data usage and the mechanisms for obtaining informed consent and addressing potential biases or unintended consequences of AI applications

and processing data sustainably. Unilever will benefit from automation for years to come thanks to its use of AI-powered technologies like RPA, ERP integration, and commitment to data quality and ethics standards.

Advanced analytics and predictive modeling could benefit Unilever's accounting and sustainability reporting methods. This could improve understanding, transparency, and stakeholder engagement. The company's stakeholder engagement and communication approach, fortified by AI-driven resolutions, epitomizes its dedication to transparency and inclusivity.

Using cutting-edge technologies and understanding stakeholders' needs has helped Unilever foster cooperation and value creation. Unilever's operating model strengthens its leadership in sustainability and sets an example for other organizations navigating 21st-century sustainable development and corporate responsibility.

Using AI technologies has changed how Unilever looks at sustainability metrics and indicators, making its efforts to measure and report on performance more accurate, reliable, and useful. By embracing a methodology rooted in discerning data analysis, Unilever can face the ever-changing difficulties of sustainable development, contributing substantially toward a robust and prosperous future for all involved.

3.4.2.1 Automation of Data Collection and Processing

In this digital age, where data are abundant and valuable, Unilever's plan to improve accounting and sustainability reporting accuracy and usefulness is based on automating data collection and processing. Introducing automation represented a significant paradigm shift in Unilever's data management approach.

RPA, which underpins the company's automation strategy, emulates human behavior and performs repetitive tasks quickly and accurately. These tasks include data input, extraction, and validation. RPA reduces the time, mental effort, and error risk of human-operated complex data collection and processing tasks for Unilever.

RPA also frees up human capital for more important projects. The strategic reallocation shows Unilever's commitment to balancing humanity and technology. RPA tools handle repetitive tasks. At the same time, the human workforce directs their attention toward complex quandaries, strategic cogitation, and the cultivation of meaningful connections with stakeholders. This concerted effort effectively enhances the organization's intellectual prowess and aptitudes.

A pivotal cornerstone of Unilever's data automation strategy lies in amalgamating its AI-driven instruments with its pre-existing ERP systems. These are where all the financial, operational, and sustainability data are kept in one place. They are very important for ensuring information flows smoothly between different business functions and applications. AI tools and ERP systems facilitate the sensible integration of knowledge from various sources (Kumar & Ravi, 2007). This simplifies good decisions.

The powerful features of ML algorithms sum up the dedication of Unilever to accurate data. When combined with anomaly detection and data cleansing techniques, these algorithms constantly check and fix the data for mistakes and contradictions (Pries & Dunnigan, 2015).

ML algorithms are dynamic tools that evolve and adapt with time. Learning from past mistakes and successes helps them identify and fix issues, improve the accuracy and reliability of data processing, and foster knowledge-based innovation. All this strengthened the foundation of Unilever's data governance framework.

3.4.2.2 Advanced Analytics and Predictive Modeling

Adding advanced analytics and predictive modeling to Unilever's accounting and sustainability reporting methods represents a huge step toward discovering deep insights with inherent value. This move beyond simple strategy shows a strong desire to use data science's huge potential to make strategic decisions and share information with stakeholders (Brown-Liburd et al., 2015; Troisi, D'Arco, et al., 2018; Troisi, Grimaldi, et al., 2018).

Unilever uses advanced analytics and predictive modeling tools. These include regression analysis to find connections between variables, time series forecasting to uncover hidden patterns in time series data, ML algorithms to learn from mistakes and adjust, and optimization models to locate solutions when quick decisions need to be made.

Every technique functions as an analysis optic, providing a singular vantage point to unravel the labyrinthine fabric of financial and nonfinancial information. A pluralistic approach allows companies to tailor their analysis methods to their data and reporting processes. This illuminates hidden patterns, trends, and connections.

The instantiation of these sophisticated techniques is interwoven within Unilever's accounting and sustainability reporting methodologies, forming an integral part of the broader ecosystem. The amalgamation affects the company and its stakeholders, symbolizing corporate disclosure transparency and inclusivity. Advanced analytics and predictive modeling make financial and sustainability performance paths easy to understand for many stakeholders (Eccles & Krzus, 2014).

In addition to their instrumental function in augmenting transparency, these techniques bestow upon Unilever the capability to peer into the future. The company uses data for more than just analysis. Predictive modeling helps "predict" the future, value risks and opportunities, and ensure business success and longevity. These advantages give companies the nimbleness to proactively address impending trials and capitalize on prospective prospects, bolstering corporate competitiveness (Malviya & Lal, 2021).

3.4.2.3 Enhanced Reporting and Disclosure

AI-driven methodologies within Unilever's accounting and sustainability reporting have transformed the organization's disclosure strategies, ensuring profundity, comprehensiveness, and fluidity. The fundamental tenets of transparency, materiality, and stakeholder inclusivity are embedded within Unilever's reporting and disclosure methodology. These principles enable corporate reporting to guide other companies and stakeholders (Eccles & Krzus, 2010).

Unilever's use of AI improved its reporting in ways that go beyond traditional methods. AI-powered solutions help companies collect and analyze data at a very fine level. This leads to more complete and detailed reports that give stakeholders a better understanding of the business's performance and prospects (Cho et al., 2020).

Furthermore, Unilever's embrace of AI technologies for data acquisition and manipulation has transformed the conventional practice of periodic reporting into more contemporary and dynamic real-time reporting. Using automated systems, Unilever creates real-time reports that give stakeholders quick and useful information.

This creates an environment that encourages stakeholders to be more responsive and make smart decisions (Chenhall & Moers, 2015). Implementing quick reporting methods acts as a discriminator in a business world that is always changing, letting organizations break down traditional barriers and maintain their advantageous position (Lambert & Sponem, 2012).

In its pursuit of comprehensive portrayal, Unilever employs AI applications to disclose both financial and nonfinancial information. By combining traditionally incompatible communication methods, the company provides a complete picture of its performance, including sustainability.

Unilever's AI-driven reporting toolkit transcends mere data aggregation and analysis, delving into the profound depths of cognitive synthesis and discernment. Unilever provides dynamic, interactive, and customizable reporting formats, catering to its stakeholders' diverse information requirements. Interactive reporting engages stakeholders and promotes discussion, improving communication and engagement (Bonsón et al., 2015).

3.4.2.4 Stakeholder Engagement and Communication

Unilever's stakeholder landscape and relationship with the company have changed due to AI-supported augmented reporting and disclosure. Investors, regulators, employees, and customers feel this paradigm shift (Chenhall & Moers, 2015).

The company's reports promote transparency, clarity, and informed decision-making. AI data collection and analysis improve Unilever's disclosures, helping investors understand the company's financial and sustainability performance.

The regulators also use augmented compliance and monitoring capabilities cultivated through the company's AI-driven reporting methodologies. Integrating AI tools with Unilever's ERP systems creates a state of financial, operational, and sustainability data integration. This makes sure that regulatory documentation is complete, accurate, and submitted on time (Kumar & Ravi, 2007). Using ML algorithms in data quality assurance also improves the truthfulness of disclosures, which builds trust between companies and the groups that regulate them (Chenhall & Moers, 2015; Ciasullo et al., 2018; Polese et al., 2019; Pries & Dunnigan, 2015).

The company's reports encourage transparency, clarity, and informed decision-making. Unilever's progress in accounting and sustainability reporting has engendered a profound imperative to scrutinize and re-examine its approaches concerning stakeholder involvement and communicative methodologies. The company has endeavored to discern and comprehend its diverse stakeholder cohorts' unique requisites, concerns, and expectations, fostering an all-encompassing and transparent dialogue. This lets Unilever tailor its communication efforts to its stakeholders' concerns and rights, promoting mutual understanding and teamwork.

Unilever communicates with many people on many levels, using channels and methods tailored to each person's needs and preferences. To exemplify, interaction with investors is nurtured through examining financial reports, active participation in earnings calls, and engagement in investor forums.

To cultivate a more expansive and inclusive relationship with its diverse stakeholders, Unilever keeps embracing conventional methodologies, namely the implementation of marketing campaigns and the utilization of various social media platforms.

However, using AI technologies has undeniably enhanced the efficiency of the organization's stakeholder service. Conversational agents and AI-powered virtual assistants make it easy for customers to get help quickly by answering their questions and easing their worries.

Finally, using NLP and sentiment analysis tools together makes it easier to look closely at feedback from stakeholders. This lets you spot new patterns and calms fears by fostering accountability (Pang & Lee, 2008).

3.4.3 Best Practices and Future Developments

Data authenticity and accuracy, serving as the lifeblood of AI-driven sustainable innovation reporting, carry a weighty responsibility. Indeed, sustainability reporting data's vast and intricate nature introduces challenges. The quality of the information, such as possible gaps, inconsistencies, and logical mistakes, could make the AI algorithms less effective, leading to wrong conclusions and bad decision-making systems (O'Dwyer & Owen, 2005).

As Unilever works to protect the integrity of information and knowledge, cleaning, validating, and verifying data become a big challenge to improve AI-enhanced reporting on sustainable innovation. Harmonizing AI technologies with existing systems and processes is another important issue.

Unilever's vast operational landscape, sprawling across multiple regions and business units, presents a mosaic of unique designs and techniques. Constructing an integrated, AI-empowered infrastructure for sustainability reporting amid such diversity is challenging (Hahn & Kühnen, 2013). For the integration process to work, many resources must be put into it, and change management must improve (Lubin & Esty, 2010).

The ethical dilemmas and regulatory adherence compound the complexity of AI-driven sustainable innovation reporting. Employing AI technologies ushers in pressing questions about data privacy, security measures, and the ethical use of data, necessitating careful consideration and prudent governance (Lee & Tajudeen, 2020). It behooves companies to stay true to stringent data governance methodologies.

The contemplation of regulatory compliance emerges as another critical motif in this growth, development, and innovation path. As a result of its roots in many local and international laws, sustainability reporting is a complicated topic that looks very different in different areas and industries (Adams & Frost, 2008). Given Unilever's sprawling global footprint, ensuring the compliance of its AI-enabled sustainability reporting with all relevant regulations forms a convoluted and challenging score on this path toward sustainability.

Based on Unilever's experience, Fig. 1 shows the connections between AI and sustainable innovation reporting.

The figure highlights how increasingly important will be to implement this emerging technology for continuous improvement, collaborative approach, transparency, and accountability.

3.4.3.1 Leveraging AI for Continuous Improvement

Unilever's endeavor to integrate AI into its sustainability reporting procedures exemplifies a profound commitment to ceaseless refinement. The constant desire to expand operations is the essence of continuous improvement because it stems from a strong conviction that even the most successful procedures have untapped potential for improvement.

The rise of AI opens up a new way to speed up the process of constantly improving sustainability reporting. This has led to a huge change in how Unilever does sustainability reporting and what effects this has on the company.

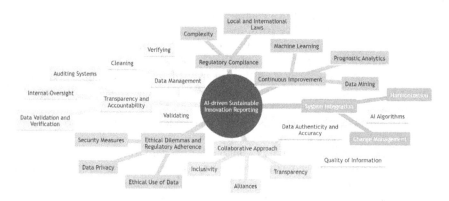

Fig. 1.   AI-Driven Sustainable Innovation Reporting.
Source: Author's elaboration.

Using AI technologies like data mining and ML algorithms, Unilever can find complex patterns and trends in large datasets (Roca & Searcy, 2012). This improves metrics and indicators over time and ensures they stay relevant, important, and aligned with shifting sustainability goals and stakeholders' expectations.

Using AI algorithms holds significant sway in detecting errors and inconsistencies within sustainability data. This facilitates the rectification of potential mistakes and enhances the overarching dependability of the data (Fedyk et al., 2022). In this way, AI plays an important part in maintaining the importance of sustainability data and creating a precise and thorough environment linked to business growth.

AI-powered prognostic analytics and benchmarking tools allow the company to compare its performance to industry peers and develop ad hoc competitive strategies (Delmas & Blass, 2010). In its commitment to sustainability, Unilever ensures that its efforts are always focused on increasing influence and efficacy by fostering innovative thought.

Additionally, using AI technologies helps bring together financial and nonfinancial performance data, which gives us a better picture of how Unilever chases success (Morrison, 2015). How Unilever's operations smoothly combine different parts allows people to think carefully about how pursuing sustainable goals affects the company's finances (Morrison, 2015).

3.4.3.2 Collaborative Approach to Sustainable Innovation Reporting

Sustainability goals require a coordinated and cooperative approach involving many people from different industries and places. Unilever's sustainable innovation reporting emphasizes transparency, inclusivity, and alliances.

Unilever's practice of sustainability reporting channels AI technologies' potential and power. The goal is to improve the system's built-in mechanisms and encourage a mutually beneficial dialogue where all stakeholders can share their thoughts.

Unilever uses cutting-edge data visualization and analytical methods to showcase its transparency and involvement in sustainability and engage its many stakeholders. AI-generated information inspires committed supporters, fostering a collective understanding and unwavering dedication to sustainable goals (Eccles & Krzus, 2010).

Unilever's collaborative modus operandi embraces a diverse spectrum of synergistic alliances with many other organizations. These entities comprise a confluence of industrial counterparts, philanthropic establishments, centers of higher learning, and universities. These alliances catalyze Unilever's capacity to allocate its resources and disseminate awareness of the importance of sustainability, thus enhancing the resounding impact of its endeavors. Better and more complex ways to view and share long-term goals, strategies, and results depend on how these groups interact (Austin & Seitanidi, 2012; Schaltegger & Wagner, 2006).

As part of this important effort, Unilever also started several projects involving many different groups to help move sustainability reporting standards and methods forward. Through its active participation in institutions like the GRI and the United Nations' SDGs, Unilever fosters the improvement of universally acknowledged benchmarks for disseminating knowledge about sustainability. This undertaking strives to cultivate a more harmonized approach to providing sustainability-related information within the industry.

Unilever's utilization of AI-based sustainability reporting technologies indicates that the company is trying to involve more than just finance, IT, and sustainability. Internal collaboration begets heightened interconnectivity within sustainability reporting. When financial and nonfinancial performance data are combined, they produce high convergence, helping better understand corporate value-creation process (Morrison, 2015).

The Unilever paradigmatic methodology shows how stakeholder involvement, symbiotic alliances, and internal harmony accelerate progress toward sustainable innovation. It illustrates how collective efforts can unlock AI's limitless potential for sustainability reporting. To that effect, Unilever can be considered a model for organizations looking to improve their sustainability reporting.

3.4.3.3 Emphasis on Transparency and Accountability

Transparency and accountability have become guiding principles in the complicated world of sustainable innovation reporting. Their consideration has improved Unilever's sustainability, credibility, integrity, and effectiveness. As a vanguard of global sustainability, the company uses AI to prioritize these principles in its pursuit of sustainable innovation reporting.

Like two threads in a braid, transparency and accountability are inseparable within the company's sustainability ethos. Unilever's decision to use AI for data validation and verification ensures that the sustainability metrics and indicators accurately reflect its performance. This shows the company is dedicated to data transparency and honesty.

Transparency is a crucial requisite of Unilever's sustainability reporting, a testament to its pledge to cultivate a milieu of openness, trust, and transparency among its stakeholders. By transforming sustainability data into a user-friendly and dynamic format, stakeholders are facilitated when evaluating the company's sustainability pursuits and their implications.

The methodologies and criteria that Unilever applies to appraise and articulate its sustainability ventures demonstrate its commitment to accountability within its reporting practices. The company has also set up a full set of internal oversight and auditing systems by incorporating the idea of accountability into its sustainability reporting guidelines. This helps to build a culture of mindfulness and accountability within the organization (Searcy, 2012).

Chapter 4

Blockchain Technology and the Quest for Decentralized Accountability

4.1 Underpinnings of Blockchain Technology in the Accounting Domain

Blockchain technology has heralded an epoch with limitless prospects and challenges within accounting (Appelbaum et al., 2022; Cai, 2021; Liu et al., 2019). The ontological basis of blockchain technology is closely linked to the progressive transformation of accounting systems (Cai, 2018; Schmitz & Leoni, 2019). Modern accounting relies on the double-entry bookkeeping system to track every transaction requiring debit and credit entry.

However, switching from traditional double-entry accounting to the advanced triple-entry accounting system is changing accounting fundamentals. Indeed, thanks to blockchain, triple-entry accounting allows adding another entry to every transaction in a distributed ledger, providing an immutable chronicle of each operation (Kokina et al., 2017). Considering a third component of each transaction improves financial statements, reduces deception, boosts stakeholder trust, and increases financial market productivity (Tapscott & Tapscott, 2016).

It becomes even more important when considering blockchain technology's impact on accounting information asymmetry (Lardo et al., 2022).

Information asymmetry causes market inefficiencies and unfair behavior. However, with its inherent capacity to offer a transparent ledger of transactions, blockchain technology fills the gap in information disparity. Blockchain technology could create a fair and efficient market by ensuring everyone has equal access to information (Spanò et al., 2022).

Within the accounting domain, this situation frequently concerns the interplay between a corporation's managers, acting as agents, and its shareholders, embodying the role of principals according to Agency theory. Blockchain's decentralization strengthens accountability and ensures the agent always serves the principal (Tapscott & Tapscott, 2016). This phenomenon may engender heightened trust and assurance in financial reporting, thereby augmenting the perceived worth and credibility of the accounting profession.

Sustainable Innovation Reporting and Emerging Technologies, 49–70
Copyright © 2024 Gennaro Maione
Published under exclusive licence by Emerald Publishing Limited
doi:10.1108/978-1-83797-739-020241004

Decentralization is crucial in blockchain. Unlike conventional centralized accounting systems, blockchain updates the registry using a distributed ledger of numerous connected nodes. Nodes copy the entire blockchain. Thus, decentralizing accounting strengthens and adapts it, reducing fraud and errors (Mougayar, 2016).

The integration of security and cryptography encapsulates the essence of blockchain in accounting. Advanced cryptography protects and links each transaction, forming a chain of virtual blocks. This cryptographic link makes the blockchain tamper-proof because altering a single transaction requires modifying all the following blocks, which is nearly impossible (Nakamoto, 2008).

Furthermore, consensus mechanisms authenticate transactions in blockchain-based accounting systems, maintaining technology integrity. Despite no central authority, these mechanisms foster system interdependence. This makes blockchain technology's potential in the accounting field even greater.

4.1.1 Key Features of Blockchain in Accounting

With its distinctive features of decentralization, security protocols, and consensus methods, blockchain technology is destined to revolutionize accounting (Coyne & McMickle, 2017; Pimentel & Boulianne, 2020). Decentralization and distributed ledger systems underpin blockchain technology. Unlike conventional centralized systems, wherein a solitary entity wields dominion over the data, blockchain functions under a decentralized paradigm.

This means that the data are stored on a large network of computers called "nodes," and each node has an exact copy of the whole record. Implementing this distributed ledger system aims to increase openness while lowering the risks of data manipulation or dishonest activities. The natural quality of this attribute shows great promise in the field of accounting, as it can lead to more accuracy and agreement in recording transactions. This boosts trust and conviction among stakeholders (Tapscott & Tapscott, 2016).

Security and cryptography, intrinsic components of blockchain technology, have profound ramifications in accounting. Utilizing blockchain entails employing sophisticated cryptographic methodologies to fortify the integrity and confidentiality of stored information. After the encryption process, each transaction becomes deeply connected to the one before, creating a logical chain of virtual blocks.

As any attempt to change or delete a transaction already recorded on the blockchain is practically impossible, this technology can assuage financial deceit and fallacies, ubiquitous apprehensions within accounting (Mougayar, 2016).

Consensus mechanisms in the realm of blockchain technology also hold paramount significance. These complex mechanisms verify transactions and protect the blockchain's inviolability. Consensus mechanisms guarantee transaction integrity and unanimity in blockchain-based accounting systems (Crosby et al., 2016).

4.1.1.1 Decentralization, Distributed Ledger Systems, Security, and Cryptography

Blockchain technology changed accounting by decentralizing power, dominion, and computational assets across interconnected nodes (Mougayar, 2016). Distributed ledgers permanently record network transactions. These features imply that every transaction is recorded with a precise time stamp and interconnected with its preceding counterpart, engendering a sequence of blocks. Replication of this chain happens across all network nodes, ensuring each participant has an exact copy of the full transactional history. This makes data unchangeable and eliminates intermediaries, saving money and time while improving efficiency (Dai & Vasarhelyi, 2017; Mougayar, 2016). The blockchain's inherent openness and inability to be changed also make people more accountable and discourage dishonest activities, which builds trust among all parties involved. Cryptography protects blockchain transactions and data (Nakamoto, 2008). It ensures legal transactions, real identities, and data security from unauthorized changes.

A distinctive identifier, commonly known as a "hash," is crafted for every block within the chain. The hash is contingent upon the intrinsic essence of the block's constituents, signifying that any modification to the data within the block will generate a distinct hash. This feature is important to the blockchain's transparency because it makes spotting any possible data breaches easy.

There are manifold potential benefits of augmented security features within blockchain-based accounting systems. The imperative for fortifying security measures has attained unprecedented significance in light of digitalizing financial transactions and records. One of the best things about blockchain-based accounting systems is that they can discourage dishonest behavior. It is very hard to change or fake transactions after they have been added to blockchain technology because of the cryptographic methods used. This boosts system trust, financial record accuracy and transparency, and fraud prevention.

4.1.1.2 Consensus Mechanisms and Trust in Blockchain-Based Accounting Systems

Consensus mechanisms are very important in blockchain networks; they are more than just functional; they make authentication and integrating transactions possible. The tools in place are crafted to ascertain unanimous consensus among all nodes within the network regarding the prevailing state of the blockchain. This maintains data integrity and coherence (Zyskind & Nathan, 2015).

Within blockchain-based accounting systems, the bedrock lies in the consensus mechanisms. They also verify and record financial transactions to ensure all parties agree before adding them to the blockchain. This method ensures financial records are accurate and unchangeable and builds trust and dependability between transaction parties (Miers et al., 2013).

In blockchain networks, one is confronted with many consensus mechanisms. Amid the prevailing methodologies, Proof of Work (PoW) and Proof of Stake (PoS) hold a primary position. Bitcoin, for example, employs the former, wherein nodes within the network engage in harmonious collaboration, unraveling mathematical quandaries. This pursuit validates transactions of utmost significance and appends validated novel blocks to the chain. When PoS is used, on the other hand, nodes confirm transactions and form new partnerships based on how many tokens they have and their willingness to "stake" those tokens as collateral (Zyskind & Nathan, 2015).

Blockchain technology has inaugurated a novel epoch of decentralized accounting systems, wherein the conventional function of intermediaries is being contested and reconfigured. This change relies on consensus mechanisms, which support transactions, maintain system integrity, and underpin blockchain technology.

According to Mougayar (2016), blockchain protocols ensure that transactions are valid and stop people from spending twice. The blockchain's security and integrity depend on this process, which brings all nodes together to agree on transaction integrity.

Consensus mechanisms play a bigger part in blockchain-based accounting systems than verifying transactions. They are also important for transparency, trust, and governance. In conventional accounting systems, trust is established through intermediaries, such as financial institutions or regulatory entities. Instead, the fact that there are no middlemen and the blockchain is decentralized, along with the fact that it cannot be changed and is open to everyone, makes users trust it.

How trustworthy and clear a blockchain-based accounting system is will depend greatly on the chosen consensus mechanism. Even though PoW systems are secure, critics say these systems waste too much energy.

PoS, on the other hand, might be more energy-efficient because it does not depend on how fast a computer is to verify transactions and add new blocks. Nevertheless, it is imperative to acknowledge that these systems are not exempt from encountering specific vulnerabilities in security (Buterin, 2014).

In the epoch of contemporary times, numerous novel consensus mechanisms have emerged, poised to tackle the difficulties that affect accounting innovations. An example is the Practical Byzantine Fault Tolerance (PBFT) algorithm that Hyperledger Fabric uses. This algorithm decides by combining voting and verification methods. This ensures that most network nodes agree on the blockchain's current state (Castro & Liskov, 1999).

Incorporating consensus mechanisms within blockchain-based accounting systems can significantly augment such systems' reliability and transparency. These mechanisms build user trust by validating all transactions and obtaining consensus from most network nodes. The consensus process, where all transactions and blocks are publicly verifiable, can also improve financial record accountability and transparency (Zyskind & Nathan, 2015).

Furthermore, utilizing consensus mechanisms within blockchain technology can profoundly enhance the system's security. Mougayar (2016) explains that the complex web of consensus mechanisms requires participants to show a precise level of commitment (regarding computer skills or financial investment), discouraging people from doing anything wrong. These mechanisms build user trust by validating all transactions and obtaining consensus from most network nodes (Zyskind & Nathan, 2015). This, in essence, nurtures a profound sense of reliance among users, for they may possess assurance in the impregnability and righteousness of the system.

4.2 Decentralized Accountability in Sustainable Innovation Reporting

Blockchain technology has engendered a profound and transformative paradigm shift in accounting, particularly in sustainable innovation reporting. The switch from centralized to decentralized accountability systems is what distinguishes this paradigm shift and profoundly influences how organizations articulate their endeavors about sustainable innovation.

The embodiment of decentralized accountability signifies a responsibility that surpasses the limitations imposed by a singular central authority. Instead, many network nodes or participants play a unique role in system safety (Bovens, 2007). The decentralized nature of this structure engenders a more fortified and enduring approach to accountability.

In sustainable innovation reporting, decentralized accountability improves transparency and credibility. Maintaining that the reporting entity cannot control or change the blockchain, which uses decentralized networks to record and verify transactions, achieves this goal. Once recorded, data are public and unchangeable, making the blockchain reliable.

Companies are asked to be more accountable and open because investors, consumers, and regulators pay increasing attention (Botti et al., 2017; Ciasullo et al., 2016; Eccles & Krzus, 2010; Troisi, Santovito, et al., 2019). The stakeholders' interest lies in discerning the organizations' contributions toward sustainable development, wherein sustainability innovation reports serve as a pivotal guide. The rise of decentralized accountability systems gives these stakeholders a solid and unquestionable source of information, ensuring that the information being shared is real (Mougayar, 2016).

Nevertheless, the journey toward decentralized accountability in sustainable innovation reporting proves to be an undertaking. The pursuit of a profound transformation in the manner in which organizations perceive and enact accountability and stakeholder engagement is imperative (Tommasetti, Del Bene, et al., 2020). This imperative lies in cultivating novel aptitudes and proficiencies, specifically in the fabric of consensus mechanisms. It also needs a regulatory environment that understands and adapts to the unique features of decentralized accountability systems (De Filippi & Wright, 2018; Maione, 2023; Tommasetti et al., 2023).

Integrating blockchain technology into sustainable innovation reporting also necessitates active participation in reevaluating established corporate strategies. Organizations should show that they are fully open to the inherent flexibility of change and can promptly adapt to the constantly shifting accounting landscape. This forces them to rethink information governance, knowledge dissemination, and stakeholder inclusion methods.

Moreover, utilizing blockchain technology in sustainable innovation reporting inevitably engenders inquiries concerning data privacy and security measures. Indeed, organizations must balance openness and privacy to satisfy stakeholder information needs while complying with data protection laws.

4.3 Blockchain as a Catalyst for Trust and Transparency

Blockchain technology embeds trust and transparency, shaping the complex dynamics of various accounting sectors (Mougayar, 2016). This, in turn, enhances stakeholders' faith in accounting systems. The ability to adhere to and validate transactions, devoid of reliance on a central governing body, gives individuals a profound sense of assurance about the exactitude of operations.

Trust is essential in transactional relationships. Decentralization eliminates duplicity and manipulation in blockchains. The consensus-based validation process builds participant trust, eliminating the need for a third party (Sadeghi et al., 2023) and benefiting accounting systems (Tapscott & Tapscott, 2016).

Blockchain technology's profound influence further improves transparency, a key element of trust. All network participants can see blockchain transactions. This attribute gives the system unprecedented transparency. From start to finish, the transaction is transparent. This ensures everyone has equal information throughout the process. Openness in accounting systems helps keep people accountable and follow regulators' rules.

Blockchain-based smart contracts increase transparency by automating regulations. Automating this process reduces human error and ensures everyone understands the agreement, fostering clarity and trust (Buterin, 2014).

4.3.1 Challenges and Limitations of Blockchain in Promoting Trust and Transparency

Blockchain technology fosters trust and transparency in accounting, but drawbacks also exist, including the interplay between technological intricacies and the concern for scalability. As a decentralized ledger, the intrinsic essence of blockchain demands considerable computational prowess and storage capability (Kshetri, 2018).

The blockchain constantly grows in size and computational power. This growth may make the system less flexible, causing transaction processing and validation delays. This can be a serious problem in those sectors where efficient transactions ensure product quality (Kshetri, 2018).

Furthermore, the difficult integration between ERP systems and blockchain intensifies these challenges. Conventional ERP techniques, commonly employed by numerous organizations, cannot easily accommodate revolutionary blockchain technology. Thus, organizations must either outsource the development of supply chain–specific applications or establish a new in-house development framework (Kshetri, 2018). Each alternative presents obstacles.

Outsourcing engenders the potential for privacy leakage risks, necessitating the organization to bestow trust upon third-party services for storing and managing its data. Alternatively, organizations must commit to long-term investment by training current employees or hiring skilled professionals with the right skills (Kshetri, 2018).

Scalability allows a system to perform well as its inputs grow. This causes more issues, including interoperability, which requires blockchain systems to work together seamlessly. Lack of interoperability standards may keep blockchains in "silos," making them harder to use (Kshetri, 2018).

Ultimately, the difficulty surrounding data integrity also poses another challenging obstacle. The blockchain technology makes it difficult to change or revise data. Integrating blockchain technology may be more harmful than advantageous if a supply chain partner opts to employ an undependable system to document information. As Kshetri (2018) noted, the blockchain's immutability does not guarantee data accuracy or reliability.

Blockchain technology implementation also requires considering regulatory and ethical issues. Despite making things clearer and easier to track, blockchain technology is decentralized, and this feature raises serious data privacy and security concerns.

Moreover, blockchain's regulation remains embryonic as diverse jurisdictions embrace disparate norms and rules governing its utilization. Regulatory heterogeneity can create uncertainty and significant obstacles for companies operating across jurisdictions.

4.4 Case Study: De Beers Group and the Tracr Blockchain Platform

The De Beers Group is the leader in the diamond industry. It boasts a luxury history extending beyond a century. Cecil Rhodes, an entrepreneur from England dedicated to diamond extraction in South Africa, founded this company in 1888 (Epstein, 1982). Over time, exploiting the Rothschild family's influence, he acquired several mining companies, considerably strengthening De Beers' position in the diamond industry.

During the early 20th century, under the guidance of Ernest Oppenheimer, De Beers embraced a strategic approach to market control that would subsequently shape its overarching business paradigm throughout a significant portion of the century. De Beers upheld price stability through the influence of supply and demand dynamics, perpetuating its hegemony within the global diamond market (Even-Zohar, 2002).

Notwithstanding, the latter portion of the 20th century bore witness to significant metamorphoses within the diamond industry, presenting obstacles to De Beers' dominion over the market. More people protested the Central Selling Organization's monopoly as Russia and Australia found new diamond deposits. De Beers slowly lost its market dominance (Bieri, 2016). In light of these changes, De Beers shifted from a market control approach to one centered on demand generation. This transformation entailed substantial investments in marketing and branding endeavors to invigorate consumer desire for diamonds (Zimnisky, 2016).

In contemporary times, De Beers has also encountered escalating attention to its activities' environmental and social repercussions. In particular, the apprehension that the commerce of diamonds has generated for several reasons, prompting appeals for augmented transparency and accountability within the distribution network (Le Billon, 2008).

Indeed, despite appearances, the diamond industry is beset with challenges endured throughout the ages, calling for high levels of accountability. One of the biggest challenges is the black-market exchange of "blood diamonds." In some cases, the gemstones are extracted from regions embroiled in armed conflict and utilized to fund insurrections against established governmental entities. Therefore, extraction may involve human rights violations, labor exploitation, and environmental degradation (Le Billon, 2008). Despite widespread efforts to stop this illicit trade, such as implementing the Kimberley Process Certification Scheme, conflict diamonds remain a significant issue (Bieri, 2016).

An important problem concerns the diamond's journey, which involves many stages and participants, from its beginnings in a mine to its market launch. This complex web of processes and individuals renders ascertaining a diamond's provenance and guaranteeing its adherence to ethical sourcing practices a stiff challenge (Hilson & McQuilken, 2014).

The diamond industry is also confronted with substantial challenges stemming from environmental concerns. The extraction of diamonds often correlates with ecological problems, encompassing deforestation, soil degradation, and water contamination (Hilson, 2002). Moreover, diamond extraction is energy-intensive and emits many greenhouse gases (Ali et al., 2017).

The emergence of synthetic diamonds poses yet another severe obstacle to industry development. This alternative to diamond mining supports ethics and sustainability because lab-grown diamonds have the same chemical makeup as natural diamonds. However, these synthetic gems raise concerns about market saturation and the diamond's symbolic value (Zimnisky, 2016), risking undermining the industry's profitability.

Given all these criticalities, De Beers has been exploring and testing an innovative approach to enhance accountability in its sustainable innovation reporting by implementing blockchain technology. The case of the De Beers Group and its Tracr platform attests to how this technology can be harnessed to tackle the difficulties prevailing in the diamond industry.

4.4.1 Research Design

A comprehensive investigation was undertaken using secondary data analysis to scrutinize the implementation of blockchain technology within the diamond industry. De Beers and its Tracr blockchain platform were considered a case study to analyze the group's openness and accountability, how they use tracking methods, and how important blockchain technology is to their operational framework and long-term reporting processes.

Financial and annual sustainability reports were downloaded from the company's official website to conduct the analysis. This helped people understand De Beers Group's work's economic, social, and environmental effects and how blockchain technology has helped its efforts to be more environmentally friendly. Several corporate strategy documents, encompassing mission statements, vision documents, and strategic action plans, were also scrutinized. Furthermore, an assortment of other pertinent documents were also thoroughly examined. These encompassed regulatory filings and presentations delivered by group executives at some diamond industry conferences. Table 1 elucidates the scrutinized records analyzed for this case study.

The documents were looked at using thematic analysis to find and understand patterns (themes) in qualitative data (Braun & Clarke, 2006). The process of thematic analysis encompassed six stages: familiarization with the data, generating codes, searching for themes, reviewing and refining themes, defining and naming themes, and producing the report.

The first stage involved repeated reading and immersion in the data to comprehensively understand the content, context, and underlying meanings. This process facilitated the identification of patterns and themes.

After thoroughly familiarizing oneself with the data, the texts were carefully coded using an open-coding approach. This entailed assigning descriptive labels to text segments pertinent to the research objectives. A total of 33 codes were generated, representing various aspects of blockchain application in De Beers Group's tracking practices, its benefits, and associated challenges. Table 2 provides an overview of these codes, categorized into application, benefits, and challenges.

Subsequently, the codes were scrutinized and grouped based on their similarities and relationships. This process led to the identification of six themes that provided a coherent data interpretation framework. Later, the themes were clearly defined and named to accurately represent their essence and scope. These themes served as the basis for presenting and discussing the research findings. Table 3 shows these themes, representing the critical aspects of De Beers Group's application of blockchain technology through its Tracr platform.

4.4.2 Findings and Discussion

Blockchain has started a new era with more openness, accountability, and control. This has caused major changes in many fields, including the diamond one. De Beers Group has been using blockchain technology to overcome long-standing challenges in the diamond industry, reshaping its landscape.

The De Beers Group's innovative Tracr blockchain platform significantly advances accountability and transparency within the diamond supply chain. This endeavor's evolution hallmarks were a quest for knowledge, encouraging teamwork, and cultivating an environment supportive of innovation. The intrinsic

Table 1. Data Set of the Case Study De Beers Group.

Year	Document Type	Number of Documents	Specifics
2022	Annual sustainability report	1	Comprehensive review of Tracr's impact on the diamond industry and sustainability (De Beers Group, 2022)
2021	Annual sustainability report	5	Report on the improved sustainability and accountability due to Tracr (De Beers Group, 2021)
2019	Corporate strategy document	1	Future plans for Tracr and its role in sustainability (De Beers Group, 2019)
2018	Financial report	1	Report on the positive financial impact of Tracr (De Beers Group, 2018a)
2018	Corporate strategy document	1	Strategic planning involving further development of Tracr (De Beers Group, 2018b)
2017	Financial report	1	Strategic planning involving further development of Tracr (De Beers Group, 2017)
2016	Annual sustainability report	1	Report on the improved sustainability and accountability due to Tracr (De Beers Group, 2016)
2016	Corporate strategy document	1	Detailed presentation of Tracr's impact on the diamond industry (De Beers Group, 2016)
2015	Corporate strategy document	1	Presentation on the economic benefits of Tracr in the diamond industry (De Beers Group, 2015)
2011	Assurance and compliance Supplement	1	Description of the assurance and compliance corporate efforts (De Beers Group, 2011)
2009	Annual sustainability report	1	Early discussions on the potential of blockchain for sustainability (De Beers Group, 2009)
2008	Corporate strategy document	1	Introduction of blockchain concepts in strategic planning (De Beers Group, 2008)

Table 2. Codes.

Area	Code
Application of blockchain in tracking practices	• Diamond origin verification • Supply chain transparency • Provenance tracking • Real-time tracking • Immutable record keeping • Integration with IoT devices • Use of smart contracts • Data encryption • Peer-to-peer transactions • Decentralized database • Automated processes
Benefits of blockchain application	• Enhanced transparency • Improved trust among stakeholders • Reduction in counterfeit diamonds • Efficient and accurate recordkeeping • Improved regulatory compliance • Enhanced customer engagement • Social and environmental responsibility • Reduced operational costs • Increased market share • Improved brand reputation • Enhanced security
Challenges associated with blockchain technology	• Technological complexity • Integration with existing systems • Data privacy concerns • Regulatory uncertainty • High implementation costs • Need for stakeholder education • Scalability issues • Interoperability with other blockchains • Energy consumption

(Continued)

Table 2. *(Continued)*

Area	Code
	• Lack of standardized protocols • Resistance to change

attributes ingrained within the platform, encompassing decentralization, security, and consensus mechanisms, have showcased their indispensable function in effectively tackling the quandaries about accountability within the diamond industry.

The Tracr platform has transformed the diamond industry by increasing trust and transparency in the supply chain and addressing information asymmetry and

Table 3. Themes.

Theme	Description
Blockchain-enabled transparency and trust	This theme encapsulates the enhanced transparency in the diamond supply chain made possible by blockchain technology. It includes real-time tracking, immutable recordkeeping, and provenance verification
Trust enhancement	This theme focuses on how blockchain technology has improved trust among stakeholders, including customers, suppliers, and regulatory bodies
Operational efficiency	This theme covers the improvements in operational efficiency resulting from blockchain applications, such as automated processes, efficient recordkeeping, and integration with IoT devices
Regulatory compliance	This theme pertains to the role of blockchain in facilitating improved compliance with industry regulations and standards
Social and environmental responsibility	This theme delves into how blockchain technology has enabled De Beers Group to demonstrate its social and environmental responsibility commitment
Scalability and interoperability issues	This theme concerns technical challenges, including blockchain systems' scalability and interoperability with other blockchains

Agency theory (Akerlof, 1970; Eisenhardt, 1989). Tracr makes it easier for people in the diamond industry and consumers to check the origin and quality of diamonds by creating a reliable database of transactions. Thus, ethical sourcing methods and industry confidence have improved (Le Billon, 2008).

Furthermore, the Tracr platform has been pivotal in cultivating a paradigm shift toward decentralized accountability in diamond sourcing and sustainability. Tracr helps companies demonstrate their commitment to ethical sourcing and sustainability through its involvement in sustainable innovation reporting. Moreover, the platform influences regulators and civil society organizations, fostering openness and responsibility (Bieri, 2016).

Table 4 lists the problems the diamond industry was having, how the Tracr blockchain platform was used to fix them, and the results achieved.

Table 4. The Use of Tracr Blockchain Platform in the Diamond Industry.

Challenge	Solution	Outcome
Lack of traceability	Use of blockchain for a tamper-proof and permanent record of transactions	Traceability from mine to market ensures each diamond's provenance and ethical sourcing
Lack of transparency	Use of blockchain for a transparent and accessible record of all transactions in the diamond supply chain	Increased diamond industry transparency, building consumer trust, and holding stakeholders accountable
Lack of accountability in diamond sourcing and sustainability	Use of blockchain for decentralized accountability, providing a transparent and immutable record of transactions that holds industry stakeholders accountable for their actions	Increased diamond industry accountability, promoting ethical and sustainable practices, and ensuring legal compliance
Information asymmetry and agency theory issues	Use of blockchain to reduce information asymmetry and align the interests of agents and principals	Reducing information asymmetry and aligning stakeholders' interests leads to fairer transactions and increased consumer trust and confidence

The following sections examine the Tracr platform's development, impact on the diamond industry, and role in decentralized accountability in diamond sourcing and sustainability. Furthermore, the diamond industry's problems and the Tracr blockchain platform's solutions are outlined.

4.4.2.1 The Tracr Blockchain Platform

Considering the difficulties characterizing the diamond industry, the De Beers Group undertook a great endeavor to implement Tracr. The development and use of this blockchain platform necessitated high technical skills, comprehensive industry insight, and harmonious stakeholder cooperation.

The execution of Tracr also necessitated a profound comprehension of the dynamics inherent in the diamond industry and the complex workings of blockchain technology. The platform was created after a detailed analysis of the diamond supply chain's challenges. This project examined the risks and issues at each stage of the supply chain, from diamond extraction to store sales. The goal was to learn how blockchain technology could improve diamond supply chain transparency and accountability.

De Beers Group has brought together professionals from blockchain development, the diamond industry, and the sustainability field. This team exhibited dedication to fostering collaboration with diverse industry stakeholders, including diamond producers, manufacturers, and retailers. They worked to tailor the platform to the diamond industry's complex needs.

The platform's design, prototyping, testing, and refinement occurred iteratively. The team sought industry stakeholders' input throughout development to ensure the platform's continued success. This iterative approach provided the platform's constant adaptability to the diamond industry's changing needs and complexities.

The execution of Tracr was undertaken systematically, commencing with a preliminary phase encompassing several industry stakeholders. The initial stage made real-world testing of the platform easier to assess its efficacy and impact. The platform was refined and improved based on pilot feedback until it was advanced and smooth before being made available to everyone.

The successful integration of Tracr necessitated providing comprehensive training and support to many stakeholders within the industry. This was very important for ensuring the participants understood how the platform worked and knew how to use its many features (Zimnisky, 2016).

The Tracr platform is founded upon many pivotal facets inherent to blockchain technology, namely decentralization, security, and consensus mechanisms. Every characteristic is indispensable in augmenting the diamond procurement network's transparency, reliance, and accountability.

Tracr uses a decentralized network with an unchangeable transaction ledger. The decentralization process significantly augments transparency, allowing every participant to trace a diamond's extraction path at the mine, culminating in its arrival at the market. This tracing guarantees the diamond's provenance and substantiates its ethical sourcing.

Security stands as an additional pivotal facet within the Tracr platform. Using cryptographic algorithms guarantees that all transactions are safeguarded and impervious to tampering. Every diamond is bestowed with an exclusive digital identification, entwined with distinctive characteristics encompassing carat weight, chromatic hue, and optical purity. The digital label is encrypted and then stored in the blockchain, ensuring a strong and unchangeable record of the diamond's unique qualities and journey. More than that, the platform uses advanced security protocols, like multi-signature wallets and two-factor authentication, to make it even harder for people to get in without permission (Zyskind & Nathan, 2015).

Consensus mechanisms also play a pivotal role in facilitating the Tracr's functioning. These mechanisms verify every transaction, preventing fraud and protecting blockchain data. Compared to many other blockchain systems, Tracr uses a better version of the PoS consensus mechanism that is scalable and more energy-efficient (Kiayias et al., 2017). Within the PoS mechanism, the selection of validators to generate a novel block is contingent upon their stake in or possession of tokens within the blockchain. This design fosters a climate that rewards virtuous conduct while discouraging malevolent behaviors (Buterin & Griffith, 2017).

The platform's decentralization, security, consensus mechanisms, easy-to-use interface, and ongoing support from De Beers Group have made Tracr widely employed among many people and organizations in the industry.

4.4.2.2 The Impact of Tracr on the Diamond Industry

Introducing the De Beers Group's Tracr platform has had a profound and far-reaching influence on the diamond industry. Tracr made today's diamond business more conscious of its ethical implications (Bieri, 2016). It has successfully addressed information asymmetry and Agency theory to improve trust and transparency. The latter within the diamond supply chain is paramount. First, it makes proving a diamond's origin easier by ensuring it was sourced ethically and avoiding any links to conflict zones. This matter assumes paramount significance given the persistent apprehensions surrounding the commerce of blood diamonds, which have been associated with transgressions against human rights and the deterioration of the environment (Le Billon, 2008).

Tracr allows for ascertaining the trajectory of a diamond's journey from its inception in the mine to its ultimate vacation in the market. This accomplishment has given people in the diamond industry and picky customers a new sense of security. It lets them verify a diamond's origin, encouraging ethical sourcing practices.

Transparency, in essence, assumes paramount significance when safeguarding a diamond's inherent excellence and worth. No reliable way to verify a diamond's qualities increases the risk of fraud and misrepresentation, which damages trade trust. The Tracr platform tackles this problem by furnishing a secure and unalterable ledger of a diamond's distinctive characteristics, encompassing its carat weight, color, and transparency.

Trust is another pivotal constituent within the tapestry of the diamond supply chain, necessitating numerous intermediaries' involvement. The industry's stakeholders trust the Tracr platform because all participants have access to a shared, unalterable ledger of transactions. This technological advancement has facilitated the execution of trades, rendering them more streamlined and productive.

With its decentralized and transparent ledger, the platform has also played a pivotal role in mitigating the inherent information asymmetry prevalent within the diamond industry. Tracr ensures that everyone involved gets an equal share of information by giving everyone access to a safe, unchangeable ledger that records the path and properties of a diamond. This fosters an increase of transparency and trust, cultivating a fairer and more proficient milieu for market operations (Mougayar, 2016).

The platform also minimized the problems related to the Agency theory, which concerns principal–agent relationships between diamond buyers and sellers. With a robust mechanism to ascertain the provenance and caliber of diamonds, Tracr reduces the peril of adverse selection and moral hazard. Adverse selection manifests itself when agents possess exclusive knowledge that eludes the grasp of principals. In contrast, a moral threat materializes when agents engage in actions that deviate from the optimal interests of their principals (Eisenhardt, 1989; Nakamoto, 2008).

4.4.2.3 Decentralized Accountability in Diamond Sourcing and Sustainability

The Tracr platform has been pivotal in cultivating a paradigm shift toward decentralized accountability in diamond sourcing and sustainability. Its involvement in sustainable innovation reporting has attained this accomplishment, influencing stakeholders and the wider diamond industry.

The pivotal function of Tracr in sustainable innovation reporting highlights blockchain technology's capacity to enhance corporate social responsibility (CSR). As an important part of CSR, sustainable innovation reporting includes showing how well a company does in areas like where diamonds come from, how they are extracted, and how they ethically sell them.

Tracr, with its transparent ledger of transactions, has undeniably augmented the potential for sustainable innovation reporting within the diamond industry. The platform affords a verifiable chronicle of a diamond's journey from the mine to the market, empowering companies to responsibly highlight their dedication to ethical sourcing and sustainability. This fits the growing focus on openness in Environmental, Social, and Governance (ESG) reporting, as stakeholders look for reliable information about a company's monetary and nonmonetary achievements (Eccles & Serafeim, 2013).

Tracr's involvement in sustainable innovation reporting encompasses the far-reaching ramifications of the diamond industry for society at large. By making a clear record of where diamonds come from and where they go, Tracr gives companies the power to show their commitment to developing sustainable mining methods, which helps achieve larger societal goals, such as the United Nations SDGs. This concurs with the burgeoning acknowledgment of companies' pivotal role in promoting sustainable development (Bieri, 2016).

The Tracr platform's influence on stakeholders and the wider diamond industry is manifold. It has transformed relationships between industry, consumers, regulators, and civil society organizations. Tracr helps diamond miners, manufacturers, and retailers find diamond origins professionally. This has augmented the establishment of trust among industry participants and decreased the peril of fraudulent activities and evil behaviors. Tracr has shown industry participants the ability to manifest their dedication to ethical sourcing and sustainability principles through a steadfast transaction ledger. This has engendered a notable increase in the company's reputation and competitiveness.

Tracr has reassured consumers of the ethical provenance and quality of the diamonds they procure. Consumers can make smart decisions thanks to the platform, which gives them clear information about a diamond's history and unique features. This increases their trust and confidence in the diamond trade, consistent with the burgeoning consumer inclination toward transparency and accountability in the goods and services they procure.

Tracr has also helped regulators and civil society organizations. It enables regulators to enforce laws by recording all transactions. Meanwhile, it has empowered civil society groups to hold industry players accountable for their actions and methods.

4.4.3 Best Practices and Future Developments

The utilization of the Tracr platform by De Beers provides interesting insights into applying blockchain technology within multifaceted and geographically widespread sectors. These insights encompass technical, operational, regulatory, and ethical aspects, as shown in Fig. 1.

Technically, Tracr's launch has shown how important technology is for monitoring decentralized transactions. Cryptography, especially public-key cryptography, is the best way to secure and verify data transparency (Narayanan et al., 2016). Also, the consensus mechanisms used in Tracr – PoW and especially PoS – have become important for ensuring that transactions are real and that the ledger stays consistent. These protocols ensured everyone agreed on the ledger's state and avoided possible double-spending or fraud (Mougayar, 2016).

Tracr showed how difficult managing massive amounts of data in a blockchain system is. Every transaction expands the blockchain, requiring lots of storage and powerful computers. Scalability was an issue because the system needed to handle more transactions while maintaining performance and security (Croman et al., 2016).

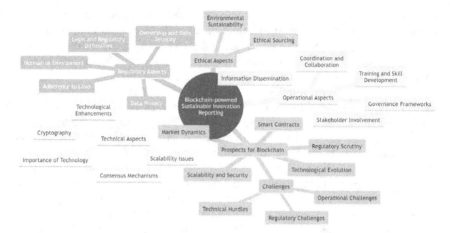

Fig. 1.   Blockchain-Powered Sustainable Innovation Reporting.
Source: Author's elaboration.

To fix these issues, it became imperative to devise ingenious resolutions and continuously pursue progressive technological enhancements. For instance, techniques such as sharding, separating the blockchain into smaller, simpler pieces, and off-chain transactions, which conduct some trades outside the blockchain, were investigated to increase scalability (Zamani et al., 2018). Similarly, sophisticated data compression methods and simplified data structures were implemented to address the expanding data.

Operationally, the deployment of Tracr has underscored the imperative of efficient coordination and harmonious collaboration among diverse stakeholders within the industry. Tracr's success was contingent upon the dynamic involvement of many stakeholders, encompassing miners, manufacturers, retailers, and consumers. Each supply chain member assumed a unique role within the diamond industry, and their cooperative efforts proved crucial in creating comprehensive and reliable documentation of diamonds' journeys.

Nevertheless, cultivating such a collaboration did not occur without encountering obstacles. The diamond industry exhibits notable fragmentation and heterogeneity, wherein various participants frequently possess divergent interests and objectives. Getting past these differences required creating governance frameworks that could balance the different interests of all the parties involved and encourage them to work together. These structures encompass mechanisms to facilitate decision-making, resolve conflicts, and align incentives to ensure the platform's seamless operation.

The deployment of Tracr has also highlighted the importance of transparency and fast information dissemination among industry stakeholders. Participants openly and promptly disseminate information in light of the platform's inherently decentralized nature and scalability challenges. The integrity and dependability of this necessary data depended on how much the participants wanted to build a climate of trust and cooperation among their peers in the same industry. This task is arduous in competitive business landscapes (Nakasumi, 2017).

The implementation of Tracr has also underscored the imperative for continuous training and the cultivation of aptitude among the various stakeholders within the industry. Blockchain technology has ushered in novel methodologies and protocols that necessitate a discernible degree of technical understanding. A basic requirement for optimal platform use is ensuring all participants have the necessary skills and knowledge (Atzori, 2015).

From the regulatory point of view, the implementation of Tracr has also underscored the importance of a favorable normative environment. Tracr offers many insights into navigating the complex relationship between technology, law, and governance. Utilizing blockchain technology within the diamond industry, specifically in sustainable innovation reporting, has prominently brought many legal and regulatory difficulties. These concerns encompass a broad spectrum, from data privacy and safeguarding intellectual property to confidentiality laws and regulations (Zetzsche et al., 2018).

The introduction of Tracr has emphasized data privacy as a paramount regulatory concern. Because blockchain records cannot be changed, keeping and protecting sensitive data has become the biggest concern. The platform's use of blockchain technology has also raised questions about ownership and data security. These issues required a deep analysis of intellectual property law and robust methods to protect organization (De Filippi & Wright, 2018).

Adherence to laws and regulations posed an additional regulatory obstacle. De Beers and its partners must follow many laws and regulations across jurisdictions because the diamond industry is global. This required vigilantly monitoring rule changes, enforcing them, and communicating with authorities (Zetzsche et al., 2018).

As an important part of Tracer's implementation process, talking with policymakers and regulators to create an open and supportive regulatory environment was seen as necessary.

Finally, the use of Tracr has also highlighted the significance of ethical sourcing and sustainability within the diamond trade. The platform strengthens De Beers' reputation and competitiveness by demonstrating its commitment to these principles. However, that project showed how difficult it is to verify blockchain data while ensuring trust (Eccles & Serafeim, 2013).

Ethical sourcing within the diamond industry is a multifaceted plight with challenges, including blood diamonds, the exploitation of child labor, and the harmful environmental impact. The incorporation of Tracr has given De Beers a formidable instrument to highlight its dedication to ethical sourcing. The platform allows De Beers to demonstrate its ethical and responsible sourcing by tracking every diamond from the mine to the customer. This enabled De Beers' to compete successfully in a scope where discerning consumers favor ethically procured commodities.

Environmental sustainability emerges as an additional paramount ethical quandary within the diamond industry. In most cases, diamond extraction and processing destroy habitats, pollute water, and release harmful carbon emissions. The integration of Tracr has allowed De Beers to manifest its dedication to environmental sustainability, as it now possesses the means to present an account of its ecological impact. This transparency mechanism made it easier for the company to build deeper relationships with its stakeholders while also motivating the company to improve its environmental performance.

4.4.3.1 Prospects for Blockchain in the Diamond Industry

The diamond industry has many exciting prospects for blockchain technology and vice versa. The advent of diamond blockchain technology presents a novel paradigm for the proficient administration and authentication of transactions within the intricate diamond supply chain. This innovative solution emerges as a beacon of hope amid the industry's arduous battle with challenges about traceability, transparency, accountability, and the pervasive problem of information asymmetry.

To date, the challenges of scalability and security persist as considerable obstacles. More blockchain transactions mean more requirements. Blockchain requisitions are paramount in upholding stakeholders' confidence in challenging environments and successfully navigating and resolving challenges.

A major issue is ensuring that blockchain platforms grow to serve more users while performing well (Mougayar, 2016). Moreover, in light of blockchain platforms' escalating intricacy and adaptability, safeguarding their integrity and invulnerability is progressively tricky. Keeping blockchain data private is more important than ever due to rising cyber threats (Zetzsche et al., 2018).

Integrating blockchain technology within the diamond sector transcends mere conformity to prevailing fashions. It responds smartly to market dynamics, discerning consumer demands, and regulatory pressures. The diamond industry has changed dramatically due to the digital revolution and societal norms. People today are more conscious of their consumer choices' moral consequences. Picky buyers always want to know where their diamonds come from and expect conflict-free, ethical sources (Mougayar, 2016).

The automatic, unchangeable record of all transactions makes blockchain ideal for this need. Regulators worldwide scrutinize the diamond industry over conflict diamonds and ethical mining concerns. Blockchain helps diamond companies comply with regulations and avoid penalties (Zetzsche et al., 2018).

One forthcoming trajectory pertains to the progressive metamorphosis of blockchain technologies and protocols. As technology matures, blockchain platform scalability, security, and interoperability will inevitably witness marked enhancements.

Scalability holds paramount importance in technology, and blockchain, without a doubt, is not exempt from this imperative. As the diamond industry progressively embraces blockchain technology, the amplitude of transactions documented on the blockchain will indubitably experience a surge. Blockchain platforms must be scalable to handle more transactions at peak performance. Scalability improvements will also speed up diamond tracking from mining to market, providing a more timely and accurate account of the transactions. This measure shall augment the traceability of diamonds, thereby fortifying consumers' trust in the ethical provenance of these precious gemstones.

The security domain is poised to undergo substantial progress in the foreseeable future. Due to its advanced cryptographic methods and consensus mechanisms, blockchain technology is secure. Nevertheless, as the technological landscape evolves, we can confidently envision a forthcoming progression in fortifying security attributes within blockchain platforms. These additions will protect the nature and privacy of recorded information, maintain trust, and comply with data privacy laws. Security improvements will make cyberattacks and data breaches easier to prevent.

Interoperability stands as an additional pivotal domain of progress. As the diamond industry traverses the path of digitization and interconnectivity, the imperative for interoperability amid diverse blockchain platforms will assume ever greater significance. Interoperability improves blockchain platforms, making data transfer between diamond supply chain parts easier. This will improve the supply chain and provide a complete view of each diamond's life cycle. Interoperability will also enable the integration of blockchain technology with other emerging technologies like AI and the IoT, creating new diamond industry innovation and value creation opportunities (Zetzsche et al., 2018).

Moreover, we can predict the evolution of increasingly refined smart contracts, embody self-execution, and inscribe the agreement's terms into code. Smart contracts can automate many procedures within the diamond supply chain. This reduces the need for intermediaries, boosts efficiency, and guarantees agreement fulfillment.

Smart contracts that can handle more transactions and agreements will emerge as technology matures. For example, smart contracts can automate the process of certifying precious stones. The relevant certification data are written onto the blockchain ledger on the diamond, ensuring it meets the requirements. This could make the certification process more efficient and trustworthy.

A smart contract gives the seller ownership and financial proceeds after a diamond sale. It saves money and time and avoids nonremittance or no-receipt. Supply-and-demand-based real-time pricing can make smart contracts more flexible (Buterin, 2014). Smart contracts also possess the inherent capacity to ensure adherence to ethical sourcing and sustainability standards. For example, a smart contract can be programmed to categorically decline any diamond transaction that fails to adhere to the explicitly outlined principles of ethical sourcing and sustainability. This would furnish a helpful instrument for ensuring adherence to these standards and exacting responsibility from industry stakeholders for their conduct (Eisenhardt, 1989).

Blockchain technology can benefit the diamond industry, but many challenges must be overcome. The problems listed above come from different technology, operations, and rule areas. Scalability and security remain technical hurdles.

Blockchain transactions require more computing power and storage space, so ensuring blockchain platforms can grow while still working perfectly and efficiently is crucial (Mougayar, 2016). Moreover, in light of blockchain platforms' escalating intricacy and adaptability, safeguarding their integrity and invulnerability is progressively tricky. Due to rising cyber threats, blockchain data privacy is crucial (Zetzsche et al., 2018).

Operational challenges also need to be faced to standardize data recording practices. Given the diverse stakeholders involved in the diamond supply chain, achieving consensus on standardized data recording practices is complex. Keeping people's trust and making the blockchain a reliable source of information requires correct, consistent, and complete data (Tapscott & Tapscott, 2016).

A high obstacle also pertains to regulatory challenges. Blockchain technology has caused many legal and regulatory issues in data privacy, intellectual property, and compliance. Successfully addressing these complex matters necessitates a profound comprehension of the regulatory scope. With blockchain technology's rapid development, regulatory changes require constant monitoring and adjustment (Zetzsche et al., 2018). Miners, manufacturers, retailers, and regulators must collaborate to face these challenges (Mougayar, 2016).

Chapter 5

The Internet of Things and Its Impact on Sustainable Innovation Reporting

5.1 The Inquiry Into the Internet of Things (IoT) in Accounting

The IoT has highly boosted technological progress, affecting many fields, including accounting (Zhang, Gu, et al., 2023). It connects devices into a single network, from simple household items to complex industrial machinery. This complex network enables unprecedented information sharing and connection.

The IoT's potential goes beyond data collection and analysis. It includes providing real-time insights and allowing companies to deal with financial patterns and outliers quickly. This real-time feature can completely change financial forecasting and risk management. It gives companies a flexible and advanced tool for planning their finances and making strategic decisions (Ahmad Zaidi & Belal, 2018).

The IoT can increase accounting transparency and trust (Rejeb et al., 2019), helping with problems like financial fraud and wrong information by showing clear and accurate pictures of financial transactions. Increased transparency may improve adherence to financial regulations and standards, boosting the accounting industry's credibility.

The IoT is a valuable instrument for accountants in financial data aggregation and examination. By using automated data collection methods, the IoT lowers the risk of mistakes made by humans and simultaneously improves the efficiency of data collection. It also enhances financial analysis by providing timely information. This lets accountants make thoughtful decisions on time.

The IoT is more than just technology; it is a powerful force changing many professions, including auditing and assurance services. Making remote auditing feasible, IoT devices give auditors ubiquitous access to and careful analysis of financial data. This improves auditing efficiency and flexibility (Crabtree et al., 2016).

Furthermore, the IoT can augment the evaluation of potential hazards within auditing and assurance services. IoT devices' expeditious provision of real-time data allows auditors to discern and promptly address financial perils.

Sustainable Innovation Reporting and Emerging Technologies, 71–94
Copyright © 2024 Gennaro Maione
Published under exclusive licence by Emerald Publishing Limited
doi:10.1108/978-1-83797-739-020241005

This could improve risk management and risk management methods, improving assurance services.

5.2 The Revolutionary Potential of the IoT in Sustainable Innovation Reporting

The IoT has the vast potential to completely change the scope of sustainable innovation documentation because it can connect different devices and make it easier to send modern information. The IoT's inherent potential resides in providing accurate, timely, and comprehensive data, enhancing the caliber and integrity of documentation about sustainable innovation.

The multifaceted nature of the IoT in sustainable innovation reporting is undeniable. On the one hand, it can augment data collection and monitoring, thereby endowing companies with abundant contemporary data about their sustainability performance. This facilitates monitoring corporate advancement toward their sustainability objectives, discerning the domains necessitating refinement, and enabling informed decision-making regarding enhancing sustainability endeavors.

Conversely, the IoT can expedite the amalgamation and scrutiny of data, empowering companies to comprehend their sustainability endeavors comprehensively. Therefore, this can lead to more thorough and accurate reporting of sustainable innovations, which makes those reports more reliable and honest.

Furthermore, the IoT can potentially propel advancements in sustainable innovation reporting. Companies can provide real-time sustainability reporting by using data from IoT devices. This makes the reports timelier and more functional. Moreover, the IoT can increase stakeholder engagement and communication, furnishing stakeholders with expeditious and precise insights into a business's sustainability performance. This can engender confidence and cooperation among companies and their stakeholders, thereby augmenting the efficacy of sustainable innovation reporting.

However, incorporating the IoT into sustainable innovation reporting is not bereft of its intrinsic intricacies. One of the foremost challenges resides within the domain of data security and the safeguarding of personal privacy. It is essential to consider propositions that aim to modify the security dynamics prevalent in cyberspace.

According to this idea, using the IoT to report sustainable innovations needs robust data security protocols to protect the privacy and accuracy of sensitive information about sustainability. The difficulty of standardization and interoperability also presents a challenge.

Kitchin (2014) says that mixing digital devices and infrastructure in cities, called "smart urbanism," makes people worry about how well the devices and infrastructure will work together. The idea behind this proposition is that including IoT technology in reports on sustainable innovation requires efforts to make sure that all IoT devices and infrastructure work together smoothly (D'Aniello et al., 2016; Malik et al., 2022).

5.2.1 IoT-Driven Innovations in Sustainable Innovation Reporting

The emergence of the IoT has ushered in a novel epoch of ingenuity in sustainable reporting, thereby revolutionizing the methodologies organizations employ to amass, scrutinize, and disseminate data about sustainability. The IoT has changed the usual static and intermittent reporting into a continuous process that affects many people, such as companies, regulators, investors, and society.

The advantages of contemporary sustainability reporting are indeed diverse. Utilizing such a system for corporate entities allows for enhanced efficacy in administering and overseeing their sustainability endeavors. This enables them to discern and rectify quandaries expeditiously, optimize the utilization of resources, curtail expenditures, and enhance operational efficacy. It also raises their sense of accountability and openness, improving their standing and stakeholder relations.

Real-time sustainability reporting gives regulators a higher level of dependability and contemporaneity as a basis for overseeing compliance with environmental and social regulations. This makes it easier to implement enforcement measures and make adequate policies. It offers many timely and intricate ESG data points for investors and fortifies risk mitigation endeavors.

Even in public discourse, it is imperative to acknowledge that disseminating corporations' sustainability performance fosters an environment of heightened transparency. This empowers people to make informed choices as discerning consumers, diligent employees, and responsible citizens (Kitchin & Dodge, 2011).

The emergence of the IoT has ushered in novel opportunities for stakeholder involvement and discourse, thereby revolutionizing sustainable innovation reporting. By establishing connectivity between ordinary objects and the vast expanse of the internet, the IoT empowers them with the extraordinary faculties of perception, retention, and computation. Because of this, it has the potential to completely change how stakeholders interact with organizations and their efforts to be sustainable (van Deursen & Mossberger, 2018).

The IoT can enable enhanced stakeholder engagement and communication using interactive reporting platforms and tools. Real-time information and insights from these platforms help stakeholders make smart decisions and have meaningful conversations with organizations (Polese et al., 2021; Troisi, Grimaldi, et al., 2019). Real-time data from IoT devices can help stakeholders track an organization's environmental performance, including carbon emissions, energy use, and waste production. This enables stakeholders to oversee the organization's ecological sustainability endeavors vigilantly. This significant degree of transparency augments trust and cultivates more robust relationships among organizations and their stakeholders.

Furthermore, the IoT can bestow upon stakeholders the means and knowledge essential for their active engagement in an organization's endeavors toward sustainability. Some examples of stakeholders are people who can use IoT-enabled devices to carefully monitor their impact on the environment or participate in collecting data. Active engagement in this endeavor can augment stakeholders' perceptions of ownership and dedication toward the organization's sustainability objectives.

5.2.2 Issues and Limitations of the IoT in Sustainable Innovation Reporting

Despite its vast array of prospects for augmenting sustainable innovation reporting, the IoT is not devoid of challenges and constraints. The advent of the IoT has inaugurated an epoch characterized by unparalleled proliferation and data interchange. In addition to providing invaluable insights for sustainable innovation reporting, the data above simultaneously elicit profound apprehensions about data security, privacy, and ownership.

Data integrity and confidentiality are paramount concerns within the expanse of the IoT landscape. Cyberattacks could compromise the data IoT devices collect and transfer. Numerous IoT devices lack comprehensive security measures, often prioritizing functionality and cost-effectiveness over the imperative aspect of safeguarding data integrity. This unfortunate tendency consequently amplifies the vulnerability to potential breaches (Roman et al., 2013).

The IoT is not devoid of apprehensions about privacy, which indeed assume significant proportions. IoT devices' ubiquitous data collection capabilities could accidently expose sensitive information, raising questions about privacy rights (Weber, 2010). Matters of ownership also manifest themselves as impediments. Many sources, networks, and systems transmit data, making its ownership and use challenging to determine (Perera et al., 2017).

These issues require an integrated approach. To protect IoT devices from cyberattacks, encryption and authentication must be integrated. Anonymization and differential privacy preserve an individual's data while allowing it to be used for sustainable innovation and comprehensive reports. In this regard, clear data ownership policies turn out to be essential.

Data security, privacy, and ownership are also crucial in sustainable innovation reporting. The data companies collect and share often includes sensitive information about their work, profits, and environmental impact. Keeping these data safe goes beyond legal and ethical obligations. Data and privacy breaches can damage a company's reputation and finances, so companies must take precautions.

Furthermore, data ownership holds significant relevance within sustainable innovation reporting. These reports often use data from IoT devices, sensors, and other data acquisition tools. Uncertainty about data ownership and legal reporting practices complicates the issue and affects report integrity, trustworthiness, and validity.

5.2.3 Standardization and Interoperability Challenges

The IoT is an expeditiously progressing domain where increasingly tools, platforms, and applications are devised and implemented. The wide range of this diversity is both a strength and a weakness. It makes it hard to achieve uniformity and complete compatibility. Not having standards and protocols could lead to fragmentation, making it harder for devices and systems to communicate effectively. This holds particular relevance within sustainable innovation reporting, where the seamless amalgamation and analysis of data from diverse sources is paramount.

Standardization in the IoT means carefully seeking and following moral guidelines and detailed specifications that control the complex ways that devices and systems "talk" to each other and work together. These standards encompass data formats, communication protocols, and device interfaces. The fundamental aim of standardization lies in guaranteeing interconnectivity among devices and systems, regardless of the producer or the specific technologies utilized. This issue is critical when reporting sustainable innovation, where combining and carefully reviewing data from different sources is necessary to make beneficial decisions (Bandyopadhyay et al., 2011).

However, achieving standardization in the IoT presents an arduous task. Developing standards for all situations is challenging due to the large number of devices, platforms, and applications and their requirements and restrictions. IoT standards must constantly be improved to keep up with cutting-edge innovations, resulting in different device or application criteria.

This complicates the interoperability environment (Bandyopadhyay et al., 2011). Interoperable systems and devices work together without problems using different technologies or standards. For the IoT, interoperability is essential because it lets devices and systems share data. However, IoT interoperability is difficult. Each device, platform, and application has its technologies and standards, making it challenging to integrate them. Without universal criteria, devices and systems may only interact with a few others. This makes data analysis and integration harder.

Numerous strategies have been proposed to tackle these challenges effectively. One viable methodology entails the utilization of middleware. Middleware is a connecting line that allows different devices and systems to work together smoothly. It hides the complexity of the underlying technologies and standards. Although it comes with a corresponding increase in complexity and susceptibility to potential vulnerabilities, the expansion of interoperability holds enormous potential for advancement.

Semantic web technologies can help everyone understand the IoT. With a common language for describing devices, information, and conditions, these technological advances can help people live peacefully in different settings. Still, these technological advances are limited and ongoing, raising concerns about their growth and usefulness (Bandyopadhyay et al., 2011).

5.3 Social Perspectives of the IoT in Accounting Practices

The emergence of the IoT has significant ramifications for accounting, particularly the social dynamics inherent within the profession. Integrating IoT technology into accounting requires a considerable workforce and skill set change. Pereira and Romero (2017) say the shift to automated and data-driven processes requires workers with better technical and analytical skills.

The conventional function of accountants is transformation, wherein there is an augmented focus on the discernment, analysis, and strategic deliberation of data. The aptitude to comprehend and harness the potential of IoT technology is swiftly evolving into an indispensable skill set within professional expertise.

The impact of the IoT on interpersonal connections and collaborative dynamics within accounting organizations and teams is diverse. The IoT's increased interconnectedness and data dissemination may improve teamwork and collaboration. Moving toward automated processes may require teams to find new ways to manage and cooperate. According to Voss and Hsuan (2009), integrating the IoT into accounting requires technical knowledge and skill to navigate the complex web of changing interpersonal dynamics.

Providing adequate support to the accounting workforce during the transition toward practices enabled by the IoT is an imperative and pivotal aspect to be carefully considered. Pereira and Romero (2017) and Voss and Hsuan (2009) noted that the above transition involves more than just learning new technical skills; it also requires a significant shift in thinking and working style. There is a considerable chance that reskilling programs and career advancement opportunities will make this process much more manageable. This will help accountants get used to the new demands of their jobs and make the most of IoT technology.

IoT technology integration requires accounting firms to foster collaboration and flexibility. According to Pereira and Romero (2017), incorporating the IoT into the accounting field requires a flexible and agile methodology and an openness to adopting novel technologies and modes of operation. Collaboration and flexibility are essential to this culture, which can help people use IoT technology well. This will help accounting firms navigate the challenges and opportunities of this new technology.

Finally, thinking about digital inclusion and access becomes essential when considering how to use IoT technology in accounting in a way that works well with everything else. The paramount challenge lies in guaranteeing equitable access to the vast array of opportunities the IoT presents for all constituents of the accounting profession, including those from marginalized and underrepresented communities. To successfully navigate this challenge, society must work together on several levels, from making detailed organizational protocols and methods to implementing broad societal and policy measures.

5.3.1 Impact on Workforce and Skill Requirements

Integrating IoT technology within accounting necessitates a workforce with refined proficiency in traversing the intricate digital terrain. This paradigm shift includes using new tools and profoundly understanding how these technologies affect accounting methods in a broader sense. As Pereira and Romero (2017) pointed out, the rise of Industry 4.0 needs competent workers to understand and manage complex systems, of which the IoT is crucial.

In the present milieu, the notion of digital literacy assumes utmost significance. In this contemporary era, it has become increasingly inadequate for accountants to possess proficiency in solely utilizing particular software tools. Conversely, practitioners must cultivate a more comprehensive comprehension of digital technologies and their ramifications in accounting. As Pereira and Romero (2017) explained, this means comprehending the complex processes by which IoT devices create, collect, and analyze data and being aware of the vast effects of using these data to help make strategic decisions.

Furthermore, integrating IoT technologies into accounting practices inherently calls for a paradigm shift toward fostering collaborative and interdisciplinary work environments. Accountants must collaborate proficiently with information technology experts, data scientists, and other stakeholders to harness the complete capabilities of IoT technologies. This endeavor necessitates not solely the acquisition of technical prowess but also cultivating adeptness in effective communication and harmonious collaboration (Pereira & Romero, 2017).

The advent of IoT-enabled accounting practices engenders profound ramifications for education and training (Loia et al., 2016) within the accounting profession. Traditional accounting education has emphasized technical skills. Reassessing these methods may require a mix of digital literacy, data analysis, and strategic thinking. Due to technological advancement, lifelong learning and professional development will become more critical (Pereira & Romero, 2017).

The advancement of Industry 4.0, as expounded upon by Pereira and Romero (2017), underscores the imperative for a labor force with the insight to comprehend and address complex systems. Accountants must be proficient in new technologies like AI and machine learning as IoT-enabled accounting methods become more common. For instance, the position of Chief Robotics Officer (CRO) is a testament to the burgeoning array of roles manifesting within this milieu. Robotics, AI, human factors modeling, and human–machine interaction will improve IoT-powered accounting systems (Pereira & Romero, 2017).

This compels us to reconsider conventional accounting positions and the requisite competencies indispensable for their successful execution.

Digital accounting evolves. Accountants now go beyond numbers. It requires data interpretation, strategic collaboration, and technological navigation. The IoT creates a massive network of connected devices and systems that generate data for smart decisions (Visvizi & Troisi, 2022). Accountants must understand the technology and be able to analyze complex data sets to use this enormous amount of data (van Deursen & Mossberger, 2018).

The IoT is a complex technology that works autonomously, and that must be understood and managed. This requires skills like technical expertise, deep thinking, and data analysis. Accountants must understand technology's complex implications, benefits, and risks. One must be able to make wise decisions based on IoT data and communicate those decisions to the organization.

The IoT is not a stagnant or unchanging technological phenomenon. It continually undergoes evolution as novel contrivances, frameworks, and applications are incessantly engendered. Accountants must adapt to these changes by learning new skills and reviewing their knowledge. In addition, individuals must be able to predict forthcoming advancements and grasp their potential ramifications for their respective organizations and accounting methodologies.

The burgeoning trend toward a workforce that is increasingly proficient in technology and possesses a heightened aptitude for analysis carries profound implications for accounting education and training. Accountancy education has traditionally focused on financial reporting and auditing. However, these traditional teaching methods may not meet field needs. Accounting education must also assimilate facets of information technology, data analysis, and strategic decision-making. It is recommended that accountants get thorough training that covers how to use IoT technologies and manage and understand them.

As technology is more integrated into accounting, the human element may become less important. However, Voss and Hsuan (2009) assert that interpersonal skills and relationships remain essential even in a world where extensive digitization is pervasive. Even in the accounting field, where technological advancements have a growing influence, the ability to eloquently convey ideas, foster harmonious cooperation, and adeptly address interpersonal complexities remains essential.

The rise of "Service Encounter 2.0" provides an interesting way to think about how to understand the complicated nature of these interactions (Larivière et al., 2017). In this paradigm, technology serves as a catalyst, either enhancing or supplanting the presence of service personnel while concurrently nurturing interconnectivity within networks. The personnel and clientele assume the pivotal positions of facilitator, visionary, orchestrator, and discriminator. The transition in societal roles underscores the paramount significance of interpersonal aptitude within the context of the contemporary digital epoch. In an age where technology permeates our lives, organizations must still include humans.

In accounting, with the increasing integration of technology into accounting practices, the essence of these interpersonal interactions will probably transform. As an illustration, utilizing IoT technologies can enable a greater prevalence of telecommuting, potentially reshaping the intricacies of collaborative efforts within teams. Accountants may need to cultivate novel proficiencies to foster fruitful collaboration within a virtual milieu. As IoT technologies automate many tasks, accountants may spend more time on client tasks. Such a shift in focus would necessitate cultivating and honing robust communication acumen and fostering interpersonally adept abilities in relationship-building.

Furthermore, integrating IoT technologies into accounting practices may impact the power dynamics permeating accounting organizations. People adept at using and understanding new technologies may gain power and influence. This has the potential to engender conflicts or tensions among teams or departments. In light of this, accounting professionals must cultivate aptitudes for deftly maneuvering these latent power dynamics.

5.3.2 Influence on Interpersonal Relationships and Collaboration

The IoT has transformed our cognitive and interactive relationship with our environment. This transformation affects our personal and professional lives. In accounting, people are increasingly interested in and integrating the IoT's growing importance and appeal for personal connections and group projects.

Integrating IoT technologies into accounting practices can reconfigure the dynamics of interpersonal connections within accounting organizations and teams. The conventional paradigm of the service encounter, predicated upon immediate vis-à-vis engagements between service providers and clientele, is being supplanted by what Larivière et al. (2017) designate as "Service Encounter 2.0." In this novel paradigm, technology is pivotal, enhancing or supplanting personnel engaged in service provision while nurturing network interconnectivity.

Technology plays a significant role in Service Encounter 2.0. It can improve or replace service providers by enabling network interconnections. The corporate operational framework drives these technological positions. Technology can improve an asset-building business model. Innovative customer relationship management (CRM) systems demonstrate asset builders' augmentation. These technological advances allow employees to access customer profiles in real time, making identifying profitable upselling and cross-selling prospects easier and increasing conversion rates.

In the contemporary landscape, one observes a burgeoning symbiosis between smart assistants and their human counterparts, wherein the former augments the latter's capabilities in service provision (Polese et al., 2016; Troisi, Sarno, et al., 2019). Concurrently, service robots have exhibited a growing propensity to engage in collaborative endeavors with their human counterparts (Perri et al., 2020; Scarmozzino et al., 2017; Spender et al., 2017; van Doorn et al., 2017).

All this significantly affects how accounting teams and organizations work together with others. As technology permeates accounting practices, one wonders if the human element will diminish. However, notwithstanding the pervasive digitization of our contemporary milieu, it is imperative to acknowledge the enduring significance of interpersonal aptitude. This skill remains indispensable even in the accounting field, where technological advancements significantly impact the ability to convey ideas eloquently, harmoniously collaborate with peers, and address interpersonal complexities.

The IoT changes how we interact with others and our surroundings. Nevertheless, it poses novel challenges regarding managing interpersonal dynamics within a profoundly digitized milieu.

The emergence of IoT technologies can fundamentally transform the operational dynamics inherent within accounting teams. The matter transcends mere mechanization of mundane duties or the augmentation of data analytics prowess. The topic is creating a new operating paradigm with high levels of interaction and cooperation. Afy-Shararah and Rich (2018) call the paradigm Operations Flow Effectiveness (OFE). Its main principle is allocating time to increase process value and streamline material flow into and out of the conversion process. This can be seen in accounting teams' careful assignment of tasks, efficient knowledge transfer, and skillful coordination of efforts.

The impact of the IoT on interpersonal connections within accounting organizations extends beyond the confines of their internal dynamics. This development principle also applies to their interactions with external stakeholders like clients and regulatory bodies. Quickly gathering, analyzing, and sharing data can result in more satisfied customers and stronger ties with governing bodies. Nevertheless, realizing this inherent capacity is not devoid of formidable obstacles and intricacies.

The IoT generates heterogeneous data from sensors, user devices, and social media (Perera et al., 2017). If used properly, these data can reveal client behavior, preferences, and trends for accounting firms. Thus, it can boost customer satisfaction and loyalty. It would be best to have strong data governance and privacy protocols, good analysis, and cutting-edge tools to use this valuable data.

Furthermore, the IoT allows us to foster heightened transparency and accountability, fortifying affiliations with regulatory entities. By making accounting data instantly accessible through IoT technologies, it is possible to improve compliance with rules, lower the risk of fraud, and boost the credibility and dependability of accounting firms. Still, this project requires facing complicated regulatory issues and handling possible data security and privacy risks.

5.3.3 Transition for the Accounting Workforce and Culture of Collaboration and Adaptability

The change in thinking toward integrating IoT in accounting practices is an eminent transformation that necessitates considering the labor force. The emergence of the IoT within accounting compels a requisite transition toward a more sophisticated and analytical skill set. This significant change in the needed skills is a massive problem for the current workforce since many people may not have the proper technical knowledge. Moving forward, it is essential to start reskilling programs to give workers the skills to take advantage of IoT tools.

Providing career development opportunities constitutes an essential facet of bolstering the workforce during this transitional period. With the assimilation of the IoT into accounting, novel vocations and prospects will probably manifest themselves. These positions may necessitate a distinct array of aptitudes and competencies, in contrast to conventional accounting roles. Henceforth, giving the labor force ample opportunities to cultivate these aptitudes and advance in their professional trajectories is imperative.

Industry 4.0 requires organizations to promote collaboration and adaptability. Interconnectivity and automation are cultural and technological changes. The successful implementation of IoT technology in accounting firms depends on creating a work environment that values teamwork, flexibility, and lifelong learning.

Cyber-physical systems, which seamlessly integrate computation, networking, and physical processes, define the Fourth Industrial Revolution. IoT, AI, robotics, cyber security, and 3D printing are all mobile technologies. Incorporating these technological advances into accounting practices affects these establishments' operations and interactions, both internally and externally.

In this novel milieu, the virtues of collaboration and adaptability assume paramount significance. Cooperation is indispensable for harnessing an organization's collective intelligence and expertise. Its purpose lies in effectively interpreting and utilizing the copious amounts of data IoT devices generate. Furthermore, it cultivates a profound sense of collective accountability and proprietorship, augmenting employee engagement and dedication.

Fostering synergy and agility throughout the organization requires a deliberate and coordinated effort. It involves creating a welcoming, diverse environment that encourages sharing and learning. It provides many learning and development opportunities to prepare employees for a technologically advanced workplace.

Leadership assumes paramount significance in the formation and molding of this cultural milieu. Leaders must show others how to work together and adapt, creating an environment where people can try new things and learn while recognizing and rewarding those behaviors (Grimaldi et al., 2017; Pantano & Corvello, 2014). They need to clearly explain their vision and smart plan for how IoT technologies can be seamlessly integrated into accounting practices. Equally significant is their ability to actively involve and engross employees in this transformative undertaking (Corvello et al., 2012; Corvello & Migliarese, 2007).

5.3.4 Digital Inclusion and Access

The IoT raises substantial concerns about digital inclusion and accessibility, especially for marginalized or underrepresented groups. Many scholars have extensively researched the differences between people with easy access to computers and the Internet and those without.

This difference is commonly called the "digital divide." Advanced technologies like the IoT can worsen the dichotomy because they require unlimited internet connectivity and skills. Regarding accounting methods, these situations could lead to situations where some social groups cannot benefit from IoT-enabled accounting. This exclusion may manifest due to a shortage of access to the necessary technological infrastructure or a deficiency in adeptly harnessing said technology.

Furthermore, the expeditious pace of technological advancement can potentially exacerbate this disparity. IoT-enabled accounting may not benefit some groups with certain accounting methods. This exclusion may stem from a lack of access to the requisite technological resources or proficiencies to proficiently navigate said technology. This matter is of particular concern, especially considering the growing significance of analytical insight in accounting, as previously deliberated upon.

Advancing digital inclusivity and guaranteeing universal access to IoT technology are complex undertakings that necessitate collaborative endeavors across multiple domains. Degbelo et al. (2016) explain that this project is very complicated because it implies getting people involved and helping them understand their data better, combining quantitative and qualitative data, ensuring open standards are followed, creating personalized services, and making interfaces people want to use.

To begin, facilitating accessible internet connectivity at an affordable cost is essential to guaranteeing comprehensive digital integration. Nevertheless, this solitary factor fails to meet the requisite criteria. Entering individuals with the requisite aptitudes to cope with digital challenges is equally essential.

This is where training programs assume significance. These programs need to be carefully made to meet the different needs of different communities, considering things like age, level of education, and digital literacy skills (Degbelo et al., 2016).

Finally, advocating for the proliferation of diversity within accounting constitutes another pivotal facet of this pursuit. This project includes ensuring that people from all backgrounds can join the workforce and that these groups' different needs and points of view are carefully considered when IoT technologies are planned and implemented. This assumes heightened importance given the burgeoning impact of technology on our interpersonal relationships and interactions with the world at large. It is also crucial to distribute IoT-enabled accounting tasks and benefits fairly.

5.4 Case Study: Bosch and the IoT for Sustainable Innovation Reporting

Bosch's technological journey began in 1886 in Stuttgart, Germany, at Robert Bosch's workshop (Herzig et al., 2012). In the early days of electrical engineering and the growing auto industry, Bosch had a big dream that came true as they stubbornly forged ahead, constantly exploring new areas in these fields. Bosch pioneered magneto ignition devices and injection technologies for automotive systems in the early 20th century. Bosch's high-voltage magneto ignition system, introduced in 1902, revolutionized automobiles and the world (Womack et al., 1990).

Since the 20th century, Bosch has successfully established its presence in the market for household appliances by foraying into the production of refrigeration units in 1933 and then introducing washing machines in 1958. The corporation persisted in broadening its portfolio, venturing into domains encompassing power tools and security systems, thus fortifying its reputation as a versatile conglomerate.

Over the 21st century, the company strategically expanded its product and service offerings using new technologies, particularly the IoT (Bresnahan & Greenstein, 1999). Bosch also understood the need to balance economic effectiveness with the goals of environmental stewardship and social responsibility (Schaltegger & Wagner, 2006). Instead, it started working toward carbon neutrality and started using sustainability reporting at the same time.

One of the most essential ideas in Bosch's corporate philosophy is sustainability, which helped the company make smart decisions about its strategic and operational goals. The strong and deeply held belief goes beyond just following the law; it includes a responsible commitment to solving social and environmental problems. The triple-bottom-line framework suggests that Bosch is a company that takes its social, environmental, and financial responsibilities seriously by carefully combining sustainable methods (Elkington & Rowlands, 1999).

Central to Bosch's sustainability approach lies a dedication to preserving our climate and the judicious utilization of our finite resources. The company has made significant steps toward becoming carbon neutral, beyond reducing direct emissions from its operations to its entire supply chain. This goal ideally aligns with the main ideas behind the Science-Based Targets initiative. This initiative emphasizes companies' crucial role in global climate change efforts (Rockström et al., 2017).

Innovative solutions lead to Bosch's energy efficiency commitment, such as the Bosch Energy Platform, designed to optimize energy consumption within its manufacturing processes and showcase the perceived paramount importance of sustainable practices. By smartly using data and digital technologies, this project shows how Bosch is actively involved in long-term digital innovation (Lozano & Huisingh, 2011).

The company's strategic impetus toward sustainability extends beyond mere environmental stewardship, encompassing a careful consideration of social dimensions. Bosch promotes a diverse and inclusive organization. Diversity – including gender, age, nationality, and experiences – fosters creativity and innovation (Cox & Blake, 1991). Moreover, Bosch assiduously cultivates a salubrious milieu for labor and the holistic welfare of its personnel, acknowledging their irreplaceable function in the triumph of the corporation (Pfeffer, 2010).

Bosch pays attention to maintaining elevated levels of business ethics and corporate governance in governance matters. The company's code of conduct and many strict internal policies are a reliable way to ensure that laws are followed and create an atmosphere of accountability (Treviño et al., 2014).

For example, Bosch's commitment to sustainability is clear in consistently following all-encompassing sustainability reporting standards, fully supporting internationally recognized ones like the GRI and the SASB (Kolk, 2010). This accentuates Bosch's devotion to actively bolstering the United Nations' Sustainable Development Goals, strengthening its reputation as a conscientious and socially accountable entity.

5.4.1 Research Design

Bosch's integration of the IoT in sustainable innovation reporting was investigated by analyzing secondary data. Bosch's commitment to sustainability, meticulous reporting, and the profound impact of the IoT on its operational framework were examined.

Several annual sustainability reports were thoroughly analyzed. The Bosch website provided these documents, making them publicly available. A thorough analysis of the financial reports was also conducted to show Bosch's sustainability efforts and the IoT's role. Corporate strategy documents like mission statements, vision documents, and strategic action plans were deeply examined.

Various regulatory filings and presentations by Bosch executives at conferences on the IoT and sustainability were also carefully examined. It also includes corporate policy documents on IoT integration from the company's investor relations section. Table 1 lists the carefully examined documents analyzed for this comprehensive case study.

Each type of document contributed unique insights into Bosch's approach to sustainability and the role of IoT in its reporting practices. After the data was collected, it was carefully examined using the thematic analysis approach, a method widely employed in the social sciences to find, look at, and understand patterns (themes) in qualitative data (Braun & Clarke, 2006).

This process comprised six stages: immersion in the data, generation of codes, search for themes, review and refinement of themes, definition and naming of themes, and report production. In the first step, reading and immersing oneself in the data were done several times to understand the content, context, and underlying meanings entirely.

Table 1. Data Set of the Case Study Bosch.

Year	Document Type	Number of Documents	Specifics
2022	Financial Report	1	Analysis of the financial implications of further IoT integration, including impacts on profitability, cost structure, and ROI (Bosch, 2022b)
2022	Annual sustainability Report	2	Emphasizing IoT's role in sustainability efforts, detailing Bosch's progress and future commitments regarding IoT and sustainability (Bosch, 2022a)
2021	Code of conduct	3	Expounding on the principles that guide the company (Bosch, 2021)
2020	Corporate strategy document	2	Outlining strategic importance of IoT in Bosch's future plans, incorporating IoT into business and product strategies (Bosch, 2020)
2019	Financial Report	1	Detailed assessment of the financial impact of IoT implementation, including cost-saving measures and new revenue streams (Bosch, 2019)
2018	Annual sustainability Report	1	Bosch's first formal outline of IoT integration, setting up the initial structures and policies (Bosch, 2018)

The documents were subsequently coded through an open-coding approach. This entailed assigning descriptive labels to pertinent text segments relative to the research objectives. This process led to creating 18 unique codes representing different aspects of IoT use in Bosch's sustainability reporting. Table 2 provides an overview of these codes, categorized into application, benefits, and challenges.

Finally, the codes were scrutinized and grouped based on their correlations and similarities. This process led to identifying six overarching themes that offered a coherent framework for data interpretation. These themes served as the foundation for presenting and discussing the research findings. Table 3 synthesizes the themes that served as the basis for presenting and discussing the results.

5.4.2 Findings and Discussion

Bosch's IoT applications in innovative urban environments aptly tackle the diverse obstacles that urbanization presents. For example, the microclimate monitoring system effectively utilizes IoT sensors to observe and record various environmental parameters. This valuable data provides practical insights to inform and guide urban planning and public health initiatives (Bibiri & Krogstie, 2017).

Table 2. Codes.

Area	Code
Application of IoT in sustainable reporting practices	• IoT in product development • IoT in operational efficiency • IoT in customer engagement • IoT in strategic decision making • IoT in sustainability initiatives
Benefits of IoT tools	• Cost savings • Improved product quality • Enhanced customer experience • Real-time decision making • Increased sustainability
Challenges associated with IoT implementation	• Data privacy concerns • Technological interoperability issues • Regulatory compliance complexities • High implementation costs • Security vulnerabilities

Table 3. Themes.

Theme	Description
Integration of IoT in Business Processes	Bosch uses IoT in product development, operational efficiency, customer engagement, and strategic decision-making, providing a complete picture of how it is integrated into the company's business processes.
Value Creation through IoT	Bosch has benefited from IoT integration in cost savings, product quality, customer experience, and real-time decision-making. It examines IoT's tangible and intangible benefits to the company.
IoT-Driven Sustainability Initiatives	This theme examines Bosch's sustainability efforts using IoT and reporting on them. IoT applications have helped Bosch reduce its environmental impact and improve resource efficiency.
Digital Transformation and Organizational Development	This theme examines how the IoT has affected Bosch's culture, structure, and work processes. It looks at how the company manages the digital transformation and smooths the transition.
Data Governance and Management in IoT	This theme examines Bosch's IoT data governance and management strategy. Given IoT devices' massive data volumes, it discusses the company's data privacy, security, and regulatory compliance.
Innovation Strategy	This theme explains Bosch's IoT strategy, commitment to innovation, and business vision for IoT.

Additionally, Bosch's smart traffic management solutions skillfully utilize the potential of IoT technologies to optimize the complex web of vehicle motion, effectively reducing the traffic that plagues urban areas. These solutions will significantly reduce pollution, improving city life in ways never before seen (Zanella et al., 2014).

The company's "Bosch IoT Suite" initiative encapsulates its foray into the IoT space. This all-encompassing solution platform is the bedrock of Bosch's IoT services, providing many capabilities encompassing device management, analytics, and cloud services. Bosch has made a significant step toward becoming an IoT-based company through this wide range of services.

Bosch's wide range of IoT applications covers many different areas and is the basis for its ambitious goal of creating a global sphere that is seamlessly connected. These applications transcend mere displays of technological prowess, instead embodying purpose-driven innovation that harmoniously aligns with the company's aspirations for sustainability. The company uses the IoT to make manufacturing processes smarter in Industry 4.0. The Nexeed Production Performance Manager has many IoT apps that make monitoring and controlling production processes in real time easy. This makes them more efficient and reduces waste (Lasi et al., 2014).

Bosch has led IoT application development to improve connected mobility's safety, efficacy, and convenience. For instance, its predictive maintenance solutions use IoT sensors and data analytics to detect vehicle malfunctions. This improves safety and reduces downtime (Mobley, 2002). Bosch's IoT-enabled fleet management solutions improve vehicle utilization, fuel consumption, and route planning, reducing carbon emissions and contributing to sustainability (Perera et al., 2017).

Regarding smart homes, Bosch offers IoT applications that create an atmosphere of comfort, safety, and smart use of energy resources. The Bosch Smart Home Controller acts as a critical nexus, promoting the integrated coexistence of various smart devices. This clever device lets people remotely control and customize their home environment, making it more convenient and comfortable (Balta-Ozkan et al., 2013). Through energy consumption optimization, these solutions uphold sustainability, particularly the idea of energy conservation (Hargreaves et al., 2013).

Bosch's traffic management solutions optimize vehicle movement and reduce congestion using IoT technologies, improving urban life, and reducing pollution (Zanella et al., 2014). These applications show Bosch's extensive IoT landscape, but the company's efforts go beyond these domains. Bosch keeps finding new ways to use the IoT, so the number of eco-friendly uses is growing exponentially. Bosch's internet-connected processes highlight how to use digital technologies' built-in features to create a sustainable future.

Adding IoT technologies to Bosch's operations goes beyond just being a technological exercise; it becomes deeply connected with the company's overall goals for sustainability. Bosch has cleverly used the IoT's endless possibilities to live up to its motto, "Invented for Life" (Bernoff & Li, 2008).

Regarding environmental sustainability, the IoT is pivotal in Bosch's comprehensive framework for enhancing energy efficiency and undertaking proactive measures to combat climate change. Through the integration of IoT solutions into its manufacturing processes, Bosch curtails its energy consumption and effectively mitigates excessive waste generation. This endeavor showcases their commitment to environmental stewardship. It is a tangible contribution toward attaining carbon emission reduction targets. The company's IoT-enabled smart home and building solutions also significantly protect energy resources and lessen the bad effects of climate change by adjusting how much energy they use (Bibri & Krogstie, 2017).

The company's IoT-powered solutions aim to improve living standards, make communities more welcoming, and engage more people (Chourabi et al., 2012). For example, Bosch's telehealth solutions use IoT technologies to make it easier to monitor patients from afar. This makes healthcare services more accessible and improves patient outcomes overall.

Regarding economic sustainability, the IoT is the foundational pillar for Bosch's overarching vision of fostering sustainable growth. The IoT allows Bosch to be more efficient and cut costs using interconnected industrial solutions. This helps the company maintain its economic strength over time (Rüßmann et al., 2015). Furthermore, the business's cutting-edge IoT products and solutions create market differentiation and a competitive edge by meeting new customer needs. This strengthens the company's money-making ability.

Fundamentally, the IoT functions as a conduit, facilitating the realization of Bosch's sustainability aspirations. This serves as a testament to the profound influence of the IoT in fostering sustainable innovation. Through its all-encompassing IoT strategy, Bosch augments its corporate sustainability profile and makes a meaningful contribution to the broader global sustainability agenda.

5.4.2.1 Bosch's Networked Production System

Bosch's networked production system, which fits into the fourth industrial revolution, combines tangible and intangible manufacturing domains (Brettel et al., 2014). This system, a symbol of Industry 4.0, seamlessly integrates information and communication technology with industrial processes, mainly through the IoT.

Bosch's complex production system integrates IoT devices, data analytics, cloud computing, and cognitive technologies. IoT sensors collect a plethora of data from diverse junctures of the manufacturing process (Kiel et al., 2017). These data cover machinery performance, material status, energy consumption, and environmental conditions. A central system running in the cloud channels the sensors' data through meticulous analysis and interpretation (Zhou et al., 2015).

Utilizing the IoT within Bosch's interconnected production system transcends the mere acquisition of data. IoT devices allow assembly line machines and parts to communicate, creating a self-regulating and harmonious production environment (Zhong et al., 2017). The sensors also facilitate prognostic maintenance implementation. By monitoring component performance, problems can be anticipated. This reduces the need for maintenance and unexpected outages (Mobley, 2002).

Moreover, the IoT assumes a paramount role in augmenting the dexterity of Bosch's manufacturing infrastructure. The IoT speeds up decision-making and improves process efficiency. This helps the system adapt quickly to changing market demands (Zhou et al., 2015).

Bosch's networked production system also had an impact on the business's overall effectiveness and operational efficiency. According to Schmidt et al. (2015), integrating the IoT within this system has produced notable results, such as noteworthy waste mitigation and increased productivity. IoT has also improved product quality by enabling stricter quality control (Lee et al., 2014). Moreover, energy consumption fine-tuning reduces the corporate environmental impact (Hodge et al., 2014).

5.4.2.2 IoT and Bosch's Sustainable Innovation Reporting

As a pioneering purveyor of technological advancements, Bosch deftly harnesses the IoT as an indispensable instrument in its endeavors to perform sustainable innovation reporting. The IoT offers enormous opportunities to effectively understand and share important sustainability metrics and advancements in previously impossible ways. Bosch's IoT applications and efforts to report on sustainable innovation are profoundly connected and can be seen in several essential areas.

Primarily within the reporting realm, Bosch employs the IoT to acquire contemporaneous data from myriad sources across its comprehensive value chain. The utilization of IoT devices throughout Bosch's operations, encompassing the factory floor and logistics, facilitates a vast aggregation of diverse data points. Bosch's sustainability reports are built on the collected data, which provides deep insights into energy use, waste generation, and emissions. The IoT's automatic and ongoing data collection ensures Bosch's sustainability reporting's timeliness and accuracy.

The implementation of this IoT-enabled reporting system has bestowed upon Bosch a multitude of advantageous outcomes. Real-time information boosts Bosch's sustainability reports' credibility with investors, customers, and regulators. IoT also helps turn sustainability goals into real-world decisions by identifying wasted resources. Keeping a steady flow of accurate and reliable information has allowed Bosch to be aware of its progress and give a clear, backed-up account of its efforts to be more environmentally friendly.

Despite the numerous advantages, Bosch's progression toward IoT-integrated sustainable innovation reporting has encountered several obstacles. IoT device integration into existing systems is complicated and time-consuming, requiring technical expertise and high investments (Lee et al., 2014). IoT devices generate massive amounts of data, making management difficult. Bosch must navigate the complex world of data privacy, security, and ownership, especially when these issues are more critical. Also, getting deep insights from all the collected data requires advanced analytical skills, which makes the process more difficult (Borgia, 2014).

5.4.2.3 The Social Impact of Bosch's IoT Practices

Bosch's strategic investment in IoT technologies has had a significant social impact. Connecting objects, systems, and services has revolutionized smart homes, cities, transportation, and manufacturing. Lasi et al. (2014) argue that IoT-enabled services improve quality of life, safety, convenience, and sustainable growth. Thus, significant social benefits result.

For instance, the IoT-enabled solutions crafted by Bosch exemplify an effective approach toward enhancing the quality of high-end domiciles. These solutions improve home safety, energy efficiency, and resident well-being. This concerted effort ultimately culminates in ameliorating overall welfare and cultivating enhanced tranquility for individuals residing therein (Bibri & Krogstie, 2017). Bosch also implemented IoT in smart cities. Public transportation, urban infra-structure, and emergency response service improvements have improved urban residents' lives (Hollands, 2020).

The use of the IoT within the company has also engendered a metamorphosis of the labor force, thereby ushering in novel prospects. This technological revolution changes the very nature of work and the skills and abilities needed (Chui et al., 2016).

One of the most conspicuous implications of the IoT lies in the heightened imperative for technical improvements. As the IoT spreads throughout Bosch's business, all employees, regardless of job, need high technical knowledge. These factors drive efforts to improve and expand employees' digital skills (Bresnahan et al., 2002).

The rising demand for workers with advanced information technology and data analytics skills highlights this phenomenon. Bosch IoT systems generate massive amounts of data, requiring advanced analytical methods to gain insights. Thus, data science and machine learning have become highly valued, prompting Bosch to develop these skills in their employees strategically.

However, it is essential to underscore the challenges that accompany this profound metamorphosis. Learning and adapting to new situations can pressure employees, leading to opposition or disengagement. Henceforth, the management of Bosch has been compelled to devise efficacious strategies for change man-agement to aid employees in traversing this transition. These plans include comprehensive training programs, policies encouraging support, and a work environment that values knowledge and creativity.

Integrating the IoT into Bosch's operational framework has also fostered the spread of new interpersonal dynamics and cooperative endeavors. The IoT's complexity and pervasiveness have created a profoundly interconnected envi-ronment (Hinds et al., 2002).

Collaboration has evolved from a mere desirable characteristic to an indis-pensable imperative. The collaborative nature of IoT systems requires harmo-nious interaction among many interconnected devices, methods, and people (Da Xu et al., 2014). Employees must work efficiently in multidisciplinary teams, as cross-functional collaboration fosters idea sharing and improves problem-solving (Edmondson & Harvey, 2018, 2018).

In addition, the IoT has transformed Bosch's interpersonal relationships. IoT applications improve people's abilities and automate tedious tasks. This transformative phenomenon restructures the workplace, affecting colleagues' relationships.

This change in thinking also affects organizational power and hierarchies. IoT systems have created a paradigm shift, challenging established hierarchical frameworks and cultivating a milieu of transparency and decentralization. Bosch management emphasizes transparent communication, participatory decision-making, and continuous support to ease this transition.

5.4.2.4 Standardization and Interoperability Issues

As Bosch progressively assimilates IoT technologies into its operations, the difficulties of standardization assume a more conspicuous nature. The company's IoT ecosystem faces a significant challenge from IoT devices' heterogeneous operating systems, protocols, and data formats. This complex phenomenon hinders communication and data exchange between devices and compromises security and privacy (Gubbi et al., 2013).

Bosch faces significant challenges from the proliferation of IoT devices in manufacturing processes. The company must ensure that these devices, each with its own data formats and communication protocols, work seamlessly together in a unified network (Fleisch et al., 2015; Perera et al., 2017).

The endeavor at hand encompasses technical intricacies and demands a discerning strategic approach. Standardization entails considering diverse stakeholders, including manufacturers, users, and regulatory entities. Because these parties' interests may not align, this agreement requires skillful negotiation and diplomacy (Weber, 2010).

Standardization protects the IoT network and the sensitive information it manages. The presence of many IoT devices, each with unique security attributes, renders the network vulnerable to potential cyber threats (Roman et al., 2013). According to Sicari et al. (2015), adopting uniform security protocols across a wide range of IoT devices can significantly reduce these risks.

The company has developed a strategy to address interoperability, pursuing accepting global standards, actively participating in rule-setting groups, investing in flexible technologies, and always being safe. The fundamental cornerstone of Bosch's retort to interoperability quandaries lies in embracing universally acknowledged standards. Bosch carefully ensures that information can flow freely between different IoT ecosystems by carefully matching its devices with popular communication protocols like Message Queuing Telemetry Transport (MQTT) and Constrained Application Protocol (CoAP) (Kiljander et al., 2014). This method makes Bosch's technology compatible with other products and lets customers easily add IoT devices to their systems (Rosen et al., 2015).

Moreover, Bosch fervently engages in diverse global consortiums that standardize IoT technologies. Illustrative instances of such consortia encompass the Industrial Internet Consortium (IIC) and the Open Connectivity Foundation

(OCF) (Koshizuka & Sakamura, 2010). Bosch can actively establish standards through these collaborative alliances, exerting influence over IoT technology's trajectory. The company will be able to shape the future of this technology field in a way that fits well with its overall strategic goals thanks to this vital participation.

Another obstacle presents itself in the expeditious evolution of IoT technology. Given how quickly and constantly technology changes in the IoT space, standards must be made with the future in mind, ensuring they can easily incorporate new technologies and features. For a global technology pioneer such as Bosch, this necessitates the sagacity to envision forthcoming technological trajectories and the malleability to conform to evolving standards.

Including adaptable technologies within Bosch's strategic approach is a pivotal element in their concerted efforts to address the challenges posed by interoperability. Considering how quickly technology changes in the IoT space, Bosch places great importance on developing and acquiring flexible technologies that can adapt to constantly changing standards.

Bosch carefully applies the same security protocols to all of its IoT devices and emphasizes the importance of security during design due to the weaknesses of a heterogeneous IoT network.

5.4.3 Best Practices and Future Developments

The Bosch case study paints a vivid and compelling picture of the IoT's transformative potential and the critical changes it brings to the reporting field on sustainable innovation. It explains not only the delineations of the current state but also prospective paths for the future, as Fig. 1 shows.

Bosch's IoT serves as a significant example to highlight the manifold advantages and difficulties entailed in the assimilation of this emerging technology. It

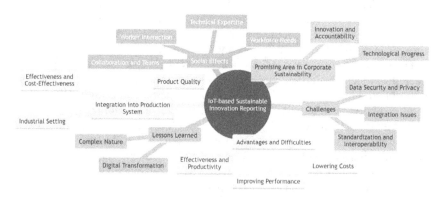

Fig. 1.   IoT-Based Sustainable Innovation Reporting.
Source: Author's elaboration.

explains how increasing effectiveness, increasing productivity, lowering costs, and improving performance can all happen as a result of technological innovation. Bosch's IoT endeavors are not exclusively fixated on operational efficacy but rather intricately interwoven with the corporation's sustainability strategy. By leveraging the IoT, Bosch has successfully optimized its sustainability reporting endeavors, engendering a seamless flow of real-time and precise data. This fortifies the company's dedication to environmental stewardship and steadfast resolve toward upholding its corporate responsibility commitments.

IoT has been carefully integrated into Bosch's production system, which shows how this technology can improve an industrial setting. The company's IoT methods have led to significant improvements in effectiveness, cost-effectiveness, and product quality, which fits with Lee et al.'s (2014) idea that IoT will bring about substantial changes in corporate production and operations management.

The social effects of Bosch's IoT practices are most noticeable in the changing needs of the workforce and the apparent effects on how workers interact with each other. The IoT allows for training workers with technical expertise (Bresnahan et al., 2002), fostering collaboration, and forming cross-functional teams (Davenport, 1990).

Bosch's progress in using the IoT for sustainable innovation reporting points to a new but promising area in corporate sustainability efforts. Eccles et al. (2014) have a positive outlook on how technological progress, like the IoT, could usher in a new era of sustainability reporting with innovation and accountability. Bosch's experience backs up this idea. It envisions a future where digital technology and sustainability are standard, changing CSR.

Bosch's encounter with the IoT further insinuates forthcoming transformations in the societal tapestry of organizations. Paradigm shifts in the workforce's needs and complex relationships between people indicate that companies will soon have to change their human resource strategies to deal with this epochal digital transformation. Bosch's empirical evidence shows how to maximize IoT's potential with technical expertise and a flexible, collaborative organizational culture.

However, this promising prospect faces challenges. Bosch's journey shows that data security, privacy, and integration are crucial issues. Moreover, the Bosch case shows how difficult it is for a multinational company to integrate IoT into its daily activities. As this case study underlines, the company's approach to the IoT includes various activities with many risks and challenges.

Indeed, Bosch faces significant standardization and interoperability issues in IoT's implementation. The company constantly tries to adopt universal benchmarks, participate in standard-setting bodies, and focus on flexible technologies, but finding global IoT standards and their problems is still difficult.

Bosch's journey into the world of IoT taught them an important lesson: the path to digital transformation is not free of obstacles. The company's commendable endeavor to harness the IoT's potential for sustainability reporting is a reminder of the complex nature of integrating technology and sustainability (Lozano & Huisingh, 2011).

In conclusion, Bosch's years of experience have helped us understand the future of IoT and sustainable innovation reporting. This is a place full of tremendous opportunities and big problems. As companies navigate the intricacies of IoT integration and strive for sustainability in this digital transformation era, the insights gleaned from Bosch's experience can prove invaluable beacons for sustainable innovation reporting.

Conclusion

When contemplating the prospective trajectory of sustainable innovation within emerging technological domains, it becomes imperative to consider the dynamic metamorphosis that artificial intelligence (AI), blockchain, and Internet of Things (IoT) may undergo over time (Visvizi et al., 2018, 2019). As elucidated in the preceding chapters, these technologies have already begun reconfiguring the accounting and sustainability reporting domains, with their impact poised to burgeon further (Kruja, 2020).

AI for sustainability reporting has many trends and innovations (Baldwin et al., 2006; Damerji & Salimi, 2021). Recent years have seen AI data collection and processing become crucial. AI algorithms can find patterns and insights in massive datasets that humans cannot (Maione & Leoni, 2021; Zhang, Zhu, et al., 2023). This is important in sustainability reporting, where data volume and complexity can be overwhelming. Nowadays, AI techniques are mature enough to assist human decision-makers in real-life situations, improving sustainability reporting data analysis efficiency and accuracy (Fedyk et al., 2022; Issa et al., 2016).

AI in sustainability reporting is more than convenience or efficiency; it redefines data analysis and decision-making. AI can find data patterns and relationships that humans cannot, changing the approach to sustainability issues (Lambin et al., 2014). Furthermore, AI can automate the data collection, diminishing the temporal and cognitive exertions in procuring the requisite information. As Han et al. (2023) note, this is especially important for sustainability reporting, where data are often scattered across different sources and formats. AI can optimize data collection, guaranteeing the comprehensive acquisition and systematic arrangement of pertinent information consistently. This leads to more accurate and reliable sustainability reports (Chui et al., 2018).

AI can also improve transparency and accountability in sustainability reporting (Leoni et al., 2021; Kokina & Davenport, 2017). AI algorithms can track and document every step of data collection and analysis, providing a detailed record of the sustainability report's production. Showing data collection, analysis, and conclusion can help stakeholders trust the news (Brynjolfsson & McAfee, 2014).

Chapter 3 discusses Unilever as an example of how AI can be used for sustainable innovation reporting. AI data collection and processing has improved

Sustainable Innovation Reporting and Emerging Technologies, 95–99
Copyright © 2024 Gennaro Maione
Published under exclusive licence by Emerald Publishing Limited
doi:10.1108/978-1-83797-739-020241006

Unilever's sustainability reporting and revealed new insights and sustainable innovation opportunities. Unilever recognized AI's potential to handle sustainability reporting's massive and complex data. Its AI algorithms can find patterns in large datasets and gain valuable insights. This has improved reporting efficiency and accuracy and revealed new sustainable innovation opportunities.

By streamlining processes and saving time, resources, and errors, Unilever automated data collection and processing with AI. Sustainability reports help the company make decisions and communicate with stakeholders. AI has improved stakeholder engagement by providing more detailed, personalized information, boosting transparency and trust. Future organizations can learn from Unilever's AI in sustainable innovation reporting. It shows how AI can transform sustainability reporting and how it can be integrated. Since AI technology is improving and sustainability reporting is becoming more critical, AI will likely be used more in this field.

Blockchain is another emerging technology that is revolutionizing sustainability reporting. Blockchain's decentralized and immutable ledger provides transparency and security by providing an unalterable record of transactions while boosting sustainability reporting trust and accountability (Cai, 2018; Schmitz & Leoni, 2019; Zhao et al., 2016). Blockchain technology can improve sustainability in reporting data integrity, verification, and traceability, ensuring that data are accurate, reliable, and verifiable. Blockchain can also track sustainability data in real time, making sustainability reporting timelier and more pertinent (Coyne & McMickle, 2017; Pimentel & Boulianne, 2020).

The future of blockchain in sustainability reporting is bright. Blockchain smart contracts can automate many sustainability reporting tasks, saving time and reducing human error. Rules-based transactions in smart contracts automate data collection, verification, and reporting (Morrison, 2016). Blockchain will also improve the sustainability reporting system's scalability and performance. Sharing and using environmental data with this technology improves sustainability reporting (Appelbaum et al., 2022; Cai, 2021; Liu et al., 2019) and democratization.

Blockchain can make sustainability reporting more inclusive and participatory by eliminating the need for intermediaries. It can empower various stakeholder groups, including consumers, investors, and regulators, to participate in the reporting process, making sustainability reporting more inclusive and relevant (Han et al., 2023; Kokina et al., 2017). Sharing economies suit blockchain (Sun et al., 2016). Real-time information sharing and digital connectivity have an impact on sustainability reporting. This technology allows real-time environmental data sharing and verification, improving sustainability reporting accountability and transparency (Lardo et al., 2022; Spanò et al., 2022).

In Chapter 4, the De Beers Group's use of the Tracr blockchain platform shows how blockchain technology can transform sustainability reporting. The diamond industry's pioneering platform helps track diamonds from mine to retail. This blockchain technology application improves diamond supply chain transparency and trust, addressing ethical sourcing and responsible business practices issues. Blockchain's decentralized ledgers record and verify every transaction and ownership transfer on Tracr. An immutable record of transactions available to all stakeholders creates unprecedented transparency, boosting consumer, retailer, and regulatory trust (Manski, 2017).

Blockchain also allows for automated data collection and reporting on the Tracr platform. Automation improves sustainability report accuracy and reliability by reducing human error and increasing efficiency (Tapscott & Tapscott, 2016). Tracr's diamond industry success inspires other transparency, trust, and accountability-challenged industries. Through blockchain-based solution development and implementation in different sectors, this technology can improve sustainability reporting.

The IoT has also created many sustainable innovation reporting opportunities and trends. Zhang, Zhu, et al. (2023) assert that an IoT network of devices, sensors, and systems can change how data are collected, processed, and reported, making sustainability reports more accurate, helpful, and efficient. Decision-making, sustainable innovation, and sustainability reporting can benefit from these insights. Hashem et al. (2016) explain that IoT and big data analytics can fundamentally change urban populations at different levels, creating a new prominent data structure for smart cities and sustainable innovation reporting.

The IoT can also help organizations integrate sustainability reporting into their operations. IoT devices and sensors in operational processes can make sustainability reporting continuous and dynamic. This change can improve sustainability reporting timeliness and responsiveness, allowing organizations to proactively and effectively identify and address sustainability issues (Teh & Rana, 2023). The IoT can also improve sustainability performance analysis.

IoT real-time monitoring and measurement can reveal an organization's sustainability performance. This capability can help organizations identify their strengths and weaknesses, set meaningful sustainability goals, and track their progress more accurately and transparently (Ahmad Zaidi & Belal, 2018). Sustainability reporting can also be made more trustworthy by the IoT. The IoT can provide a direct, unmediated data source that reduces manipulation and misrepresentation. This capability gives stakeholders confidence in sustainability reporting, which boosts their engagement and support for sustainability initiatives.

Bosch's sustainable innovation reporting using IoT is compelling, as discussed in Chapter 5. Bosch improves sustainability reporting transparency, accuracy, and timeliness by monitoring and managing energy consumption, waste generation, and other sustainability parameters in real time with IoT technologies. This case demonstrates how IoT can transform sustainability reporting and serves as a guide for other organizations.

Bosch's networked production system uses IoT technologies to provide real-time sustainability data. Bosch has reduced its environmental impact and improved sustainability by using data to identify inefficiencies and take immediate action. Bosch's IoT-driven sustainability reporting has also increased corporate social impact. Bosch engages stakeholders better by providing real-time sustainability data and promoting transparency and accountability.

Soon, smart sensors, edge computing, and 5G connectivity will further boost the IoT's sustainable innovation reporting potential. Smart sensors can monitor environmental parameters in real time, providing accurate sustainability reporting data. Edge computing reduces data transmission latency and bandwidth and improves data processing efficiency by processing data locally. With high speed and low latency, 5G connectivity can transmit and process massive amounts of data in real time, improving sustainability reporting.

In conclusion, to summarize what emerged in the theoretical discussion and analysis of the three case studies, it is possible to state that investigating how accounting has changed over time from a passive record of economic transactions to an active force shaping society is helpful to understand how this has affected sustainable innovation reporting (RQ_1). This paradigm shift has fundamentally influenced the direction of sustainable innovation reporting, creating a new narrative in the field that combines sustainability and accounting.

Accounting started as a passive economic record-keeping tool. Prehistoric societies used accounting principles for simple trade transactions, which led to the discipline. This early accounting was transactional and focused on trade equity and account balances. Double-entry bookkeeping in the late Middle Ages began accounting's historical transformation, fostering a transparent, reliable, comprehensive system that helped modern capitalism (Yamey, 1949). It also transformed the discipline from a reflective tool to a proactive force that shaped economic decision-making and social norms.

In the 19th century, modern accounting theory expanded accounting beyond economic transactions (Watts & Zimmerman, 1986). In a rapidly industrializing society, accounting norms and standards influence decision-making, corporate behavior, and societal norms (Watts & Zimmerman, 1986). Accounting became an active socioeconomic factor, shaping rather than reflecting economic and social realities.

In the second half of the 20th century, CSR led accounting to incorporate social and environmental issues, recognizing companies as social agents with broader responsibilities (Elkington & Rowlands, 1999). Accounting started to reflect this shift by developing sustainability reporting frameworks as corporations became more aware of their social and environmental responsibilities. These frameworks, such as the GRI and SASB, allowed corporations to disclose their sustainability performance, expanding accounting beyond financial reporting.

The historical transformation of accounting has also drawn attention to companies' moral duties and encouraged them to discuss their social and environmental performance. To date, the accounting profession presents opportunities and challenges for sustainable innovation reporting. The field is moving toward sustainability and innovation globally. However, obstacles intertwined with prospects (RQ_2) create a complex landscape of promise and perplexity (Kolk, 2010).

Nowadays, sustainability is prioritized and integrated into many companies' core operations. This transformative business attitude is promising for sustainable innovation reporting, requiring robust frameworks that capture a company's social, environmental, and economic impacts (Eccles et al., 2013).

However, the lack of universal sustainability reporting standards and frameworks is a significant obstacle. The GRI and SASB are voluntary, so adherence varies, and comparability across companies and industries is difficult. As a result, the lack of standardized frameworks and metrics hinders sustainable innovation reporting.

Furthermore, despite growing recognition of sustainability as a critical corporate responsibility, theory and practice remain far apart (Crane et al., 2019). Many companies claim to be sustainable but fail to incorporate it into their business strategies (Crane et al., 2019). This discrepancy limits how accounting practices and disclosures can fully reflect sustainability initiatives, making sustainable innovation reporting difficult.

To solve this problem, scholars and practitioners must constantly engage in dialogue to promote accountability, transparency, and ethical conduct through sustainable innovation reporting (RQ$_3$). This convergence can be achieved through knowledge exchange and pioneering accounting research and practice.

First, academic conferences, workshops, and seminars facilitate scholar-practitioner dialogue and knowledge exchange (Jørgensen & Messner, 2010). These forums allow practitioners to share the latest scholarly findings and academics to hear about real-world challenges. Conferences also promote idea sharing, which is essential for addressing the complexities of sustainable innovation reporting (Ahrens & Chapman, 2007).

Moreover, collaborative research projects and case studies can bridge theory and practice. Joint research projects give scholars firsthand knowledge of practitioners' operational challenges, guiding their academic research toward practical applications. The latest accounting research theories and methods can also benefit practitioners.

Scholar-practitioner collaborations should also improve and standardize sustainable reporting frameworks. Multiple frameworks with different standards cause reporting inconsistencies and comparability issues. Thus, global sustainable reporting standards should be promoted to improve sustainability disclosure transparency and comparability.

Continuous professional development and education also contribute to this convergence. The latest research can be incorporated into accounting curricula and professional training programs to prepare the next generation of practitioners for sustainable innovation reporting challenges and opportunities. Academics must also adapt their research and teaching to industry needs. Ethics, for example, is an area where scholars and practitioners must agree. Everyone needs to establish new technology ethical guidelines and talk constantly about the moral effects of accounting methods, particularly regarding sustainability reporting and new technologies. This convergence can promote a culture of ethical behavior within organizations, which is crucial for sustainable innovation reporting.

References

Abbott, L. J., Parker, S., Peters, G. F., & Raghunandan, K. (2004). Audit committee characteristics and restatements. *Auditing: A Journal of Practice & Theory*, *23*(1), 69–87.

Abernethy, M. A., & Stoelwinder, J. U. (1995). The role of professional control in the management of complex organizations. *Accounting, Organizations and Society*, *20*(1), 1–17.

Adams, C. A., & Frost, G. R. (2008). Integrating sustainability reporting into management practices. *Accounting Forum*, *32*(4), 288–302.

Adams, C. A. (2015). The international integrated reporting council: A call to action. *Critical Perspectives on Accounting*, *27*, 23–28.

Adams, R. B., & Ferreira, D. (2009). Women in the boardroom and their impact on governance and performance. *Journal of Financial Economics*, *94*(2), 291–309.

Adams, C. A., & Larrinaga, C. (2019). Progress: Engaging with organizations in pursuit of improved sustainability accounting and performance. *Accounting, Auditing & Accountability Journal*, *32*(8), 2367–2394.

Adams, C. A., & McNicholas, P. (2007). Making a difference: Sustainability reporting, accountability and organizational change. *Accounting, Auditing & Accountability Journal*, *20*(3), 382–402.

Adams, C. A., Potter, B., Singh, P. J., & York, J. (2016). Exploring the implications of integrated reporting for social investment (disclosures). *The British Accounting Review*, *48*(3), 283–296.

Adams, C., & Zutshi, A. (2004). Corporate social responsibility: Why business should act responsibly and be accountable. *Australian Accounting Review*, *14*(34), 31–39.

Adler, P. S., & Borys, B. (1996). Two types of bureaucracy: Enabling and coercive. *Administrative Science Quarterly*, *41*(1), 61–89.

Afy-Shararah, M., & Rich, N. (2018). Operations flow effectiveness: A systems approach to measuring flow performance. *International Journal of Operations & Production Management*, *38*(11), 2096–2123.

Aguilera, R. V., & Cuervo-Cazurra, A. (2004). Codes of good governance worldwide: What is the trigger? *Organization Studies*, *25*(3), 415–443.

Ahmad Zaidi, M. F., & Belal, H. M. (2018). Understanding the effects of technological advancement (IoT) on value co-creation and firm performance. *Management & Accounting Review*, 1–10.

Ahrens, T., & Chapman, C. S. (2007). Management accounting as practice. *Accounting, Organizations and Society*, *32*(1–2), 1–27.

Akerlof, G. A. (1970). The market for "lemons": Quality uncertainty and the market mechanism. *Quarterly Journal of Economics*, *84*(3), 488–500.

Alavi, M., & Leidner, D. E. (2001). Knowledge management and knowledge management systems: Conceptual foundations and research issues. *MIS Quarterly*, 107–136.

Alderman, J., & Jollineau, S. J. (2020). Can audit committee expertise increase external auditors' litigation risk? The moderating effect of audit committee independence. *Contemporary Accounting Research, 37*(2), 717–740.

Alfawaz, S., Nelson, K., & Mohannak, K. (2010). Information security culture: A behaviour compliance conceptual framework. In *Proceedings of the 8th Australasian Information Security Conference (AISC 2010)* (Vol. 105, pp. 47–55). University of Southern Queensland.

Ali, S. H., Giurco, D., Arndt, N., Nickless, E., Brown, G., Demetriades, A., Durrheim, R., Enriquez, M. A., Kinnaird, J., Littleboy, A., Meinert, L. D., Oberhänsli, R., Salem, J., Schodde, R., Schneider, G., Vidal, O., & Yakovleva, N. (2017). Mineral supply for sustainable development requires resource governance. *Nature, 543*(7645), 367–372.

Amat, O., Blake, J., & Dowds, J. (1999). The ethics of creative accounting. *Economics Working Paper, 349*, 715–736.

Anseel, F., Beatty, A. S., Shen, W., Lievens, F., & Sackett, P. R. (2015). How are we doing after 30 years? A meta-analytic review of the antecedents and outcomes of feedback-seeking behavior. *Journal of Management, 41*(1), 318–348.

Appelbaum, D., Cohen, E., Kinory, E., & Stein Smith, S. (2022). Impediments to blockchain adoption. *Journal of Emerging Technologies in Accounting, 19*(2), 199–210.

Appelbaum, D., Kogan, A., Vasarhelyi, M., & Yan, Z. (2017). Impact of business analytics and enterprise systems on managerial accounting. *International Journal of Accounting Information Systems, 25*, 29–44.

Arens, A. A., Elder, R. J., & Beasley, M. S. (2010). *Auditing and assurance services: An integrated approach*. Pearson.

Armenakis, A. A., & Bedeian, A. G. (1999). Organizational change: A review of theory and research in the 1990s. *Journal of Management, 25*(3), 293–315.

Arnold, B., & De Lange, P. (2004). Enron: An examination of agency problems. *Critical Perspectives on Accounting, 15*(6–7), 751–765.

Atzori, M. (2015). Blockchain technology and decentralized governance: Is the state still necessary? *SSRN Electronic Journal*. https://doi.org/10.2139/ssrn.2709713

Atzori, L., Iera, A., & Morabito, G. (2010). The Internet of Things: A survey. *Computer Networks, 54*(15), 2787–2805.

Austin, J. E., & Seitanidi, M. M. (2012). Collaborative value creation: A review of partnering between nonprofits and companies: Part 1. Value creation spectrum and collaboration stages. *Nonprofit and Voluntary Sector Quarterly, 41*(5), 726–758.

Baker, C. R., & Bettner, M. S. (1997). Interpretive and critical research in accounting: A commentary on its absence from mainstream accounting research. *Critical Perspectives on Accounting, 8*(4), 293–310.

Baker, C. R., & Hayes, R. (2004). Reflecting form over substance: The case of Enron Corp. *Critical Perspectives on Accounting, 15*(6–7), 767–785.

Baldwin, A. A., Brown, C. E., & Trinkle, B. S. (2006). Opportunities for artificial intelligence development in the accounting domain: The case for auditing. *Smart Systems in Accounting, Finance & Management: International Journal, 14*(3), 77–86, 100598.

Balta-Ozkan, N., Davidson, R., Bicket, M., & Whitmarsh, L. (2013). Social barriers to the adoption of smart homes. *Energy Policy, 63*, 363–374.

Bampton, R., & Cowton, C. J. (2013). Taking stock of accounting ethics scholarship: A review of the journal literature. *Journal of Business Ethics, 114*(3), 549–563.

Bampton, R., & Maclagan, P. (2005). Why teach ethics to accounting students? A response to the sceptics. *Business Ethics: A European Review, 14*(3), 290–300.

Bandyopadhyay, S., Sengupta, M., Maiti, S., & Dutta, S. (2011). Role of middleware for Internet of Things: A study. *International Journal of Computer Sciences and Engineering Systems, 2*(3), 94–105.

Barrainkua, I., & Espinosa-Pike, M. (2015). Cultural and socio-economic restrictions for the adoption of the IESBA code of ethics for professional accountants in the European countries. *European Research Studies, 18*(1), 3–24.

Barth, M. E. (2015). Financial accounting research, practice, and financial accountability. *Abacus, 51*(4), 499–510.

Barth, M. E., & Schipper, K. (2008). Financial reporting transparency. *Journal of Accounting, Auditing and Finance, 23*(2), 173–190.

Baryannis, G., Dani, S., Validi, S., & Antoniou, G. (2018). Decision support systems and artificial intelligence in supply chain risk management. In *Revisiting supply chain risk* (pp. 53–71). Springer International Publishing.

Baryannis, G., Validi, S., Dani, S., & Antoniou, G. (2019). Supply chain risk management and artificial intelligence: State of the art and future research directions. *International Journal of Production Research, 57*(7), 2179–2202.

Bass, B. M. (1985). *Leadership and performance beyond expectations.* Free Press.

Bass, B. M., & Avolio, B. J. (1994). *Improving organizational effectiveness through transformational leadership.* Sage.

Battilana, J., & Casciaro, T. (2012). Change agents, networks, and institutions: A contingency theory of organizational change. *Academy of Management Journal, 55*(2), 381–398.

Baucus, M. S., Norton, W. I., Baucus, D. A., & Human, S. E. (2008). Fostering creativity and innovation without encouraging unethical behavior. *Journal of Business Ethics, 81*(1), 97–115.

Bazerman, M. H., Loewenstein, G., & Moore, D. A. (2002). Why good accountants do bad audits. *Harvard Business Review, 80*(11), 96–103.

Bean, D. F., & Bernardi, R. A. (2007). Ethics education in our colleges and universities: A positive role for accounting practitioners. *Journal of Academic Ethics, 5*(1), 59–75.

Beasley, M. S., Carcello, J. V., Hermanson, D. R., & Lapides, P. D. (2000). Fraudulent financial reporting: Consideration of industry traits and corporate governance mechanisms. *Accounting Horizons, 14*(4), 441–454.

Beattie, V. (2014). Accounting narratives and the narrative turn in accounting research: Issues, theory, methodology, methods and a research framework. *The British Accounting Review, 46*(2), 111–134.

Bebbington, J., & Larrinaga, C. (2014). Accounting and sustainable development: An exploration. *Accounting, Organizations and Society, 39*(6), 395–413.

Bebbington, J., & Unerman, J. (2018). Achieving the United Nations sustainable development goals: An enabling role for accounting research. *Accounting, Organizations and Society, 31*(1), 2–24.

Benston, G. J., Bromwich, M., & Wagenhofer, A., & Institute of Chartered Accountants in England and Wales. (2006). Principles-versus rules-based accounting standards: The FASB's standard setting strategy. *Abacus*, *42*(2), 165–188.

Berisha, A., Kruja, A., & Hysa, E. (2022). Perspective of critical factors toward successful public–private partnerships for emerging economies. *Administrative Sciences*, *12*(4), 160.

Bernoff, J., & Li, C. (2008). Harnessing the power of the oh-so-social web. *MIT Sloan Management Review*, *49*(3), 36.

Bhimani, A., & Langfield-Smith, K. (2007). Structure, formality and the importance of financial and non-financial information in strategy development and implementation. *Management Accounting Research*, *18*(1), 3–31.

Bibiri, S. E., & Krogstie, J. (2017). Smart sustainable cities of the future: An extensive interdisciplinary literature review. *Sustainable Cities and Society*, *31*, 183–212.

Bienvenido-Huertas, D., Farinha, F., Oliveira, M. J., Silva, E. M., & Lança, R. (2020). Comparison of artificial intelligence algorithms to estimate sustainability indicators. *Sustainable Cities and Society*, *63*, 102430.

Bieri, F. (2016). *From blood diamonds to the Kimberley process: How NGOs cleaned up the global diamond industry*. Routledge.

Blei, D. M., & Lafferty, J. D. (2006). Dynamic topic models. In *Proceedings of the 23rd International Conference on Machine Learning* (pp. 113–120). Association for Computing Machinery.

Blei, D. M., Ng, A. Y., & Jordan, M. I. (2003). Latent dirichlet allocation. *Journal of Machine Learning Research*, *3*, 993–1022.

Boland, R. J., Sharma, A. K., & Afonso, P. S. (2008). Designing management control in hybrid organizations: The role of path creation and morphogenesis. *Accounting, Organizations and Society*, *33*(7–8), 899–914.

Bono, J. E., & Judge, T. A. (2004). Personality and transformational and transactional leadership: A meta-analysis. *Journal of Applied Psychology*, *89*(5), 901.

Bonsón, E., & Bednárová, M. (2022). Artificial intelligence disclosures in sustainability reports: Towards an artificial intelligence reporting framework. In *Digital transformation in industry: Digital twins and new business models* (pp. 391–407). Springer International Publishing.

Bonsón, E., Lavorato, D., Lamboglia, R., & Mancini, D. (2021). Artificial intelligence activities and ethical approaches in leading listed companies in the European Union. *International Journal of Accounting Information Systems*, *43*, 100535.

Bonsón, E., Royo, S., & Ratkai, M. (2015). Citizens' engagement on local governments' Facebook sites. An empirical analysis: The impact of different media and content types in Western Europe. *Government Information Quarterly*, *32*(1), 52–62.

Boon, H. J. (2011). Raising the bar: Ethics education for quality teachers. *Australian Journal of Teacher Education*, *36*(7), 76–93.

Borgia, E. (2014). The Internet of Things vision: Key features, applications and open issues. *Computer Communications*, *54*, 1–31.

Bosch. (2018). *Bosch annual sustainability report* [Report]. https://assets.bosch.com/media/global/sustainability/reporting_and_data/2018/bosch-sustainability-report-2018-factbook.pdf

Bosch. (2019). *Bosch financial statement* [Report]. https://www.annualreports.com/HostedData/AnnualReportArchive/b/bosch_2019.pdf

Bosch. (2020). *Bosch business strategy document* [Report]. https://assets.bosch.com/media/global/bosch_group/our_figures/pdf/bosch-today-2023.pdf

Bosch. (2021). *Bosch code of conduct* [Report]. https://assets.bosch.com/media/en/global/sustainability/strategy/vision_and_goals/bosch-code-of-business-conduct.pdf

Bosch. (2022a). *Bosch annual sustainability report* [Report]. https://assets.bosch.com/media/global/sustainability/reporting_and_data/2022/bosch-sustainability-report-2022.pdf

Bosch. (2022b). *Bosch financial statement* [Report]. https://assets.bosch.com/media/global/bosch_group/our_figures/pdf/bosch-annual-report-2022.pdf

Botosan, C. A., & Plumlee, M. A. (2002). A re-examination of disclosure level and the expected cost of equity capital. *Journal of Accounting Research, 40*(1), 21–40.

Botti, A., Grimaldi, M., Tommasetti, A., Troisi, O., & Vesci, M. (2017). Modeling and measuring the consumer activities associated with value cocreation: An exploratory test in the context of education. *Service Science, 9*(1), 63–73.

Bovens, M. (2007). Analysing and assessing accountability: A conceptual framework. *European Law Journal, 13*(4), 447–468.

Braun, V., & Clarke, V. (2006). Using thematic analysis in psychology. *Qualitative Research in Psychology, 3*(2), 77–101.

Bresnahan, T. F., Brynjolfsson, E., & Hitt, L. M. (2002). Information technology, workplace organization, and the demand for skilled labor: Firm-level evidence. *Quarterly Journal of Economics, 117*(1), 339–376.

Bresnahan, T., & Greenstein, S. (1999). Technological competition and the structure of the computer industry. *The Journal of Industrial Economics, 47*(1), 1–40.

Brettel, M., Friederichsen, N., Keller, M., & Rosenberg, M. (2014). How virtualization, decentralization and network building change the manufacturing landscape: An Industry 4.0 perspective. *International Journal of Mechanical, Aerospace, Industrial, Mechatronic and Manufacturing Engineering, 8*(1), 37–44.

Brown, H. S., de Jong, M., & Levy, D. L. (2009). Building institutions based on information disclosure: Lessons from GRI's sustainability reporting. *Journal of Cleaner Production, 17*(6), 571–580.

Brown, J., & Dillard, J. (2014). Integrated reporting: On the need for broadening out and opening up. *Accounting, Auditing & Accountability Journal, 27*(7), 1120–1156.

Brown, J., & Dillard, J. (2015). Opening accounting to critical scrutiny: Towards dialogic accounting for policy analysis and democracy. *Journal of Comparative Policy Analysis: Research and Practice, 17*(3), 247–268.

Brown-Liburd, H., Issa, H., & Lombardi, D. (2015). Behavioral implications of Big Data's impact on audit judgment and decision making and future research directions. *Accounting Horizons, 29*(2), 451–468.

Brynjolfsson, E., & McAfee, A. (2014). *The second machine age: Work, progress, and prosperity in a time of brilliant technologies.* W. W. Norton & Company.

Brynjolfsson, E., & McAfee, A. (2017). The business of AI. *Harvard Business Review, 1*, 1–31.

Buiten, M. C. (2019). Towards intelligent regulation of AI. *European Journal of Risk Regulation, 10*(1), 41–59.

Bunderson, J. S., & Sutcliffe, K. M. (2003). Management team learning orientation and business unit performance. *Journal of Applied Psychology, 88*(3), 552.

Burnes, B. (2004). Kurt Lewin and the planned approach to change: A re-appraisal. *Journal of Management Studies, 41*(6), 977–1002.

Burns, J., & Scapens, R. W. (2000). Conceptualizing management accounting change: An institutional framework. *Management Accounting Research, 11*(1), 3–25.

Busch, T., Bauer, R., & Orlitzky, M. (2016). Sustainable development and financial markets: Old paths and new avenues. *Business & Society, 55*(3), 303–329.

Busco, C., Frigo, M. L., Quattrone, P., & Riccaboni, A. (2013). Redefining corporate accountability through integrated reporting: What happens when values and value creation meet? *Strategic Finance, 8*, 183–204.

Busco, C., Frigo, M. L., & Riccaboni, A. (2013). *Integrated reporting: Concepts and cases that redefine corporate accountability.* Springer.

Bushman, R. M., & Smith, A. J. (2001). Financial accounting information and corporate governance. *Journal of Accounting and Economics, 32*(1–3), 237–333.

Buterin, V. (2014). A next-generation smart contract and decentralized application platform. *White Paper, 3*(37), 2–1.

Buterin, V., & Griffith, V. (2017). *Casper the friendly finality gadget.* arXiv Preprint. https://doi.org/10.48550/arXiv.1710.09437

Cai, C. W. (2018). Disruption of financial intermediation by FinTech: A review on crowdfunding and blockchain. *Accounting & Finance, 58*(4), 965–992.

Cai, C. W. (2021). Triple-entry accounting with blockchain: How far have we come? *Accounting & Finance, 61*(1), 71–93.

Calabrese, A., Costa, R., Tiburzi, L., & Brem, A. (2023). Merging two revolutions: A human-AI method to study how sustainability and Industry 4.0 are intertwined. *Technological Forecasting and Social Change, 188*, 122265.

Callahan, E. S., & Dworkin, T. M. (1994). Who blows the whistle to the media and why: Organizational characteristics of media whistleblowers. *American Business Law Journal, 32*(2), 151–184.

Calo, R. (2017). Artificial intelligence policy: A primer and roadmap. *UCDL Rev., 51*, 399.

Carmeli, A., Reiter-Palmon, R., & Ziv, E. (2010). Inclusive leadership and employee involvement in creative tasks in the workplace: The mediating role of psychological safety. *Creativity Research Journal, 22*(3), 250–260.

Carmona, S., & Trombetta, M. (2008). On the global acceptance of IAS/IFRS accounting standards: The logic and implications of the principles-based system. *Journal of Accounting and Public Policy, 27*(6), 455–461.

Carson, E., Fargher, N., Geiger, M., Lennox, C., Raghunandan, K., & Willekens, M. (2013). Audit reporting for going-concern uncertainty: A research synthesis. *Auditing: A Journal of Practice & Theory, 32*(1), 353–384.

Carter, D. A., Simkins, B. J., & Simpson, W. G. (2003). Corporate governance, board diversity, and firm value. *Financial Review, 38*(1), 33–53.

Castro, M., & Liskov, B. (1999). Practical Byzantine fault tolerance. In *Proceedings of the third symposium on Operating Systems Design and Implementation*, New Orleans, USA (pp. 173–186).

Chatfield, M. (1977). *A history of accounting thought.* Krieger Publishing Company.

Chenhall, R. H., & Moers, F. (2015). The role of innovation in the evolution of management accounting and its integration into management control. *Accounting, Organizations and Society, 47*, 1–13.

Cho, C. H., Michelon, G., Patten, D. M., & Roberts, R. W. (2015). CSR report assurance in the USA: An empirical investigation of determinants and effects. *Sustainability Accounting, Management and Policy Journal, 5*(2), 130–148.

Cho, S., Vasarhelyi, M. A., Sun, T., & Zhang, C. (2020). Learning from machine learning in accounting and assurance. *Journal of Emerging Technologies in Accounting, 17*(1), 1–10.

Chourabi, H., Nam, T., Walker, S., Gil-Garcia, J. R., Mellouli, S., Nahon, K., & Scholl, H. J. (2012). Understanding smart cities: An integrative framework. In *Proceedings of the 45th Hawaii International Conference on System Sciences*, Maui, HI, USA (pp. 2289–2297). IEEE.

Christensen, C. M., Ojomo, E., & Dillon, K. (2017). *The prosperity paradox: How innovation can lift nations out of poverty*. Harper Business.

Christensen, C. M., & Raynor, M. E. (2013). *The innovator's solution: Creating and sustaining successful growth*. Harvard Business Review Press.

Chui, K. T., Lytras, M. D., & Visvizi, A. (2018). Energy sustainability in smart cities: AI, smart monitoring, and optimization of energy consumption. *Energies, 11*(11), 2869.

Chui, M., Manyika, J., & Miremadi, M. (2016). Where machines could replace humans—And where they can't (yet). *McKinsey Quarterly*, 1–8.

Ciasullo, M. V., Polese, F., Troisi, O., & Carrubbo, L. (2016). How service innovation contributes to co-create value in service networks. In *Exploring Services Science: 7th International Conference, IESS 2016*, May 25–27, 2016 (Vol. 7, pp. 170–183). Springer International Publishing.

Ciasullo, M. V., Troisi, O., Loia, F., & Maione, G. (2018). Carpooling: Travelers' perceptions from a big data analysis. *The TQM Journal, 30*(5), 554–571.

Clikeman, P. M. (2009). *Called to account: Financial frauds that shaped the accounting profession*. Routledge.

Coffee, J. C. (2002). Understanding Enron: It's about the gatekeepers, stupid. *The Business Lawyer, 57*(4), 1403–1420.

Coates, J. C. (2007). The goals and promise of the Sarbanes-Oxley Act. *The Journal of Economic Perspectives, 21*(1), 91–116.

Cohen, J. R., & Holder-Webb, L. L. (2006). Rethinking the influence of agency theory in the accounting academy. *Issues in Accounting Education, 21*(1), 17–30.

Cohen, J. R., Pant, L. W., & Sharp, D. J. (1998). The effect of gender and academic discipline diversity on the ethical evaluations, ethical intentions and ethical orientation of potential public accounting recruits. *Accounting Horizons, 12*(3), 250.

Cohen, J. R., & Simnett, R. (2018). CSR and assurance services: A research agenda. *Auditing: A Journal of Practice & Theory, 34*(1), 59–74.

Coles, J. L., Daniel, N. D., & Naveen, L. (2008). Boards: Does one size fit all? *Journal of Financial Economics, 87*(2), 329–356.

Cooper, D. J., Ezzamel, M., & Qu, S. Q. (2017). Popularizing a management accounting idea: The case of the balanced scorecard. *Contemporary Accounting Research, 34*(2), 991–1025.

Cooper, L. A., Holderness, D. K., Jr., Sorensen, T. L., & Wood, D. A. (2019). Robotic process automation in public accounting. *Accounting Horizons, 33*(4), 15–35.

Corvello, V., Gitto, D., Carlsson, S., & Migliarese, P. (2012). Using information technology to manage diverse knowledge sources in open innovation processes. In *Managing open innovation technologies* (pp. 179–197). Springer Berlin Heidelberg.

Corvello, V., & Migliarese, P. (2007). Virtual forms for the organization of production: A comparative analysis. *International Journal of Production Economics, 110*(1–2), 5–15.

Covaleski, M. A., Dirsmith, M. W., & Michelman, J. E. (1993). An institutional theory perspective on the DRG framework, case-mix accounting systems and health-care organizations. *Accounting, Organizations and Society, 18*(1), 65–80.

Cox, T., & Blake, S. (1991). Managing cultural diversity: Implications for organizational competitiveness. *The Academy of Management Executive, 5*(3), 45–56.

Coyne, J. G., & McMickle, P. L. (2017). Can blockchains serve an accounting purpose? *Journal of Emerging Technologies in Accounting, 14*(2), 101–111.

Crabtree, A., Lodge, T., Colley, J., Greenhalgh, C., Mortier, R., & Haddadi, H. (2016). Enabling the new economic actor: Data protection, the digital economy, and the databox. *Personal and Ubiquitous Computing, 20*, 947–957.

Crane, A., & Matten, D. (2010). *Business ethics: Managing corporate citizenship and sustainability in the age of globalization.* Oxford University Press.

Crane, A., Matten, D., Glozer, S., & Spence, L. J. (2019). *Business ethics: Managing corporate citizenship and sustainability in the age of globalization.* Oxford University Press.

Croman, K., Decker, C., Eyal, I., Gencer, A. E., Juels, A., Kosba, A., & Wattenhofer, R. (2016, February). On scaling decentralized blockchains: (A position paper). In *International conference on financial cryptography and data security* (pp. 106–125). Springer.

Crosby, M., Nachiappan, Pattanayak, P., Verma, S., & Kalyanaraman, V. (2016). Blockchain technology: Beyond bitcoin. *Applied Innovation Review, 2*, 6–19.

Da Xu, L., He, W., & Li, S. (2014). Internet of Things in industries: A survey. *IEEE Transactions on Industrial Informatics, 10*(4), 2233–2243.

Dai, J., & Vasarhelyi, M. (2017). Towards blockchain-based accounting and assurance. *Journal of Information Systems, 31*(3), 5–21.

Damerji, H., & Salimi, A. (2021). Mediating effect of use perceptions on technology readiness and adoption of artificial intelligence in accounting. *Accounting Education, 30*(2), 107–130.

Daske, H., Hail, L., Leuz, C., & Verdi, R. (2008). Mandatory IFRS reporting around the world: Early evidence on the economic consequences. *Journal of Accounting Research, 46*(5), 1085–1142.

Davenport, T. H. (1990). The new industrial engineering: Information technology and business process redesign. *Sloan Management Review, 31*(4), 11–28.

Davenport, T. H., & Harris, J. G. (2005). Automated decision making comes of age. *MIT Sloan Management Review, 46*(4), 83–89.

Davenport, T. H., & Ronanki, R. (2018). Artificial intelligence for the real world. *Harvard Business Review, 96*(1), 108–116.

De Beers Group. (2008). *De Beers Group corporate strategy document* [Report]. https://www.debeersgroup.com/~/media/Files/D/De-Beers-Group/documents/reports/library/debeers-ofr-2008-feb-2009-pdf-downloadasset.PDF

De Beers Group. (2009). *De Beers Group annual sustainability report* [Report]. https://www.debeersgroup.com/~/media/Files/D/De-Beers-Group-V2/documents/reports/library/rts09-full-report-may-2010pdfdownloadasset.PDF

De Beers Group. (2011). *De Beers Group corporate assurance and compliance supplement* [Report]. https://www.debeersgroup.com/~/media/Files/D/De-Beers-Group-V2/documents/reports/library/rts-2011-assurance-and-compliance-supplementpdfdownloadasset.PDF

De Beers Group. (2015a). *De Beers Group strategy document* [Report]. https://www.debeersgroup.com/~/media/Files/D/De-Beers-Group-V2/documents/reports/library/report-to-society-2015pdfdownloadasset.pdf

De Beers Group. (2015b). *De Beers Group strategy document* [Report]. https://www.debeersgroup.com/~/media/Files/D/De-Beers-Group-V2/documents/reports/library/report-to-society-08-full-report-april-2009-pdf-downloadasset.PDF

De Beers Group. (2016). *De Beers Group strategy document* [Report]. https://www.debeersgroup.com/~/media/Files/D/De-Beers-Group-V2/documents/reports/library/debeers-rts-2016pdfdownloadasset.pdf

De Beers Group. (2017). *De Beers Group financial results* [Report]. https://www.debeersgroup.com/media/company-news/2017/interim-financial-results-for-2017

De Beers Group. (2018a). *De Beers Group annual sustainability report* [Report]. https://www.debeersgroup.com/~/media/Files/D/De-Beers-Group-V2/documents/reports/publications/gri-index-2016-.pdf

De Beers Group. (2018b). *De Beers Group financial results* [Report]. https://www.debeersgroup.com/media/company-news/2018/interim-financial-results-for-2018

De Beers Group. (2019). *De Beers Group financial results* [Report]. https://www.debeersgroup.com/media/company-news/2019/interim-financial-results-for-2019

De Beers Group. (2021a). *2021 sustainability: Shaping the future of the diamond sector* [Report]. https://www.debeersgroup.com/~/media/Files/D/De-Beers-Group-V2/documents/reports/insights/2021/2021-the-diamond-insight-report.pdf

De Beers Group. (2021b). *De Beers Group corporate strategy document* [Report]. https://www.debeersgroup.com/~/media/Files/D/De-Beers-Group-V2/documents/building-forever/our-journey/our-journey-vol-2.PDF

De Beers Group. (2022). *Building forever: Our 2022 sustainability report* [Report]. https://www.debeersgroup.com/sustainability-and-ethics/building-forever-reports

De Filippi, P., & Wright, A. (2018). *Blockchain and the law: The rule of code.* Harvard University Press.

De George, R. T., Li, X., & Shivakumar, L. (2016). A review of the IFRS adoption literature. *Review of Accounting Studies, 21*(3), 898–1004.

DeAngelo, L. E. (1981). Auditor size and audit quality. *Journal of Accounting and Economics, 3*(3), 183–199.

Deegan, C. (2002). Introduction: The legitimising effect of social and environmental disclosures – A theoretical foundation. *Accounting, Auditing & Accountability Journal, 15*(3), 282–311.

Deegan, C. (2017). Twenty five years of social and environmental accounting research within critical perspectives of accounting: Hits, misses and ways forward. *Critical Perspectives on Accounting, 43*, 65–87.

DeFond, M., & Zhang, J. (2014). A review of archival auditing research. *Journal of Accounting and Economics, 58*(2–3), 275–326.

Degbelo, A., Granell, C., Trilles, S., Bhattacharya, D., Casteleyn, S., & Kray, C. (2016). Opening up smart cities: Citizen-centric challenges and opportunities from GIScience. *ISPRS International Journal of Geo-Information, 5*(2), 16.

Del Bene, L., Tommasetti, A., Leoni, G., & Maione, G. (2020). How to boost environmental accounting practices: Evidence from two Italian case studies. In S. Garzella (Ed.), *Corporate social responsibility* (pp. 167–182). Franco Angeli. ISBN: 978-88-351-0509-1.

Del Bene, L., Tommasetti, A., Maione, G., & Leoni, G. (2020). The effects of OGD-based accounting practices on perceived accountability of public administrations. *Azienda Pubblica, 1*(2020), 13–28. ISSN 1127-5812.

Dellaportas, S. (2006). Making a difference with a discrete course on accounting ethics. *Journal of Business Ethics, 65*(4), 391–404.

Delmas, M. A., & Blass, V. D. (2010). Measuring corporate environmental performance: The trade-offs of sustainability ratings. *Business Strategy and the Environment, 19*(4), 245–260.

Denison, D. R., Hart, S. L., & Kahn, J. A. (1996). From chimneys to cross-functional teams: Developing and validating a diagnostic model. *Academy of Management Journal, 39*(4), 1005–1023.

DeSanctis, G., & Gallupe, R. B. (1987). A foundation for the study of group decision support systems. *Management Science, 33*(5), 589–609.

Detert, J. R., & Burris, E. R. (2007). Leadership behavior and employee voice: Is the door really open? *Academy of Management Journal, 50*(4), 869–884.

Detert, J. R., & Edmondson, A. C. (2011). Implicit voice theories: Taken-for-granted rules of self-censorship at work. *Academy of Management Journal, 54*(3), 461–488.

DeZoort, F. T., Hermanson, D. R., Archambeault, D. S., & Reed, S. A. (2002). Audit committee effectiveness: A synthesis of the empirical audit committee literature. *Journal of Accounting Literature, 21*, 38–75.

Di Vaio, A., Palladino, R., Hassan, R., & Escobar, O. (2020). Artificial intelligence and business models in the sustainable development goals perspective: A systematic literature review. *Journal of Business Research, 121*, 283–314.

Dillard, J. F., Rigsby, J. T., & Goodman, C. (2004). The making and remaking of organization context: Duality and the institutionalization process. *Accounting, Auditing & Accountability Journal, 17*(4), 506–542.

Donaldson, T., & Preston, L. E. (1995). The stakeholder theory of the corporation: Concepts, evidence, and implications. *Academy of Management Review, 20*(1), 65–91.

Douglas, P. C., Davidson, R. A., & Schwartz, B. N. (2001). The effect of organizational culture and ethical orientation on accountants' ethical judgments. *Journal of Business Ethics, 34*, 101–121.

Duan, Y., Edwards, J. S., & Dwivedi, Y. K. (2019). Artificial intelligence for decision making in the era of Big Data – Evolution, challenges and research agenda. *International Journal of Information Management, 48*, 63–71.

Duska, R. F., & Duska, B. S. (2003). *Accounting ethics.* Blackwell Publishing.

Duska, R. F., Duska, B. S., & Kury, K. W. (2018). *Accounting ethics.* John Wiley & Sons.

D'Aniello, G., Gaeta, A., Gaeta, M., Lepore, M., Orciuoli, F., & Troisi, O. (2016). A new DSS based on situation awareness for smart commerce environments. *Journal of Ambient Intelligence and Humanized Computing, 7*, 47–61.

Eccles, R. G., Ioannou, I., & Serafeim, G. (2014). The impact of corporate sustainability on organizational processes and performance. *Management Science, 60*(11), 2835–2857.

Eccles, R. G., & Krzus, M. P. (2010). *One report: Integrated reporting for a sustainable strategy*. John Wiley & Sons.

Eccles, R. G., & Krzus, M. P. (2014). *The integrated reporting movement: Meaning, momentum, motives, and materiality*. John Wiley & Sons.

Eccles, R. G., & Serafeim, G. (2013). The performance frontier: Innovating for a sustainable strategy. *Harvard Business Review, 91*(5), 50–60.

Eccles, R. G., & Serafeim, G. (2014). Corporate and integrated reporting: A functional perspective. *SSRN Electronic Journal*. https://doi.org/10.2139/ssrn.2388716

Eccles, R. G., Serafeim, G., Seth, D., & Ming, C. C. Y. (2013). The performance frontier: Innovating for a sustainable strategy: Interaction. *Harvard Business Review, 91*(7), 17–18.

Edmondson, A. (1999). Psychological safety and learning behavior in work teams. *Administrative Science Quarterly, 44*(2), 350–383.

Edmondson, A. C. (2003). Speaking up in the operating room: How team leaders promote learning in interdisciplinary action teams. *Journal of Management Studies, 40*(6), 1419–1452.

Edmondson, A. C., & Harvey, J. F. (2018). Cross-boundary teaming for innovation: Integrating research on teams and knowledge in organizations. *Human Resource Management Review, 28*(4), 347–360.

Edwards, J. R. (1989). *A history of financial accounting (RLE accounting)*. Routledge.

Eisenhardt, K. M. (1989a). Agency theory: An assessment and review. *Academy of Management Review, 14*(1), 57–74.

Eisenhardt, K. M. (1989b). Building theories from case study research. *Academy of Management Review, 14*(4), 532–550.

Eisenhardt, K. M., & Martin, J. A. (2000). Dynamic capabilities: What are they? *Strategic Management Journal, 21*(10–11), 1105–1121.

Elitaş, C., & Üç, M. (2009). The change on the foundations of the Turkish accounting system and the future perspective. *Critical Perspectives on Accounting, 20*(5), 674–679.

Elkington, J., & Rowlands, I. H. (1999). Cannibals with forks: The triple bottom line of 21st century business. *Alternatives Journal, 25*(4), 42.

Epstein, E. J. (1982). *The diamond invention*. Hutchinson.

Erhardt, N. L., Werbel, J. D., & Shrader, C. B. (2003). Board of director diversity and firm financial performance. *Corporate Governance: An International Review, 11*(2), 102–111.

Even-Zohar, C. (2002). *From mines to mistress: Corporate strategies and government policies in the international diamond industry*. Mining Journal Books.

Everett, J., Neu, D., & Rahaman, A. S. (2006). The global fight against corruption: A Foucaultian, virtues-ethics framing. *Journal of Business Ethics, 65*, 1–12.

Eynon, G., Hill, N., & Stevens, K. (1997). Factors that influence the moral reasoning abilities of accountants: Implications for universities and the profession. *Journal of Business Ethics, 16*(12/13), 1297–1309.

Ezzamel, M., Robson, K., Stapleton, P., & McLean, C. (2007). Discourse and institutional change: 'Giving accounts' and accountability. *Management Accounting Research, 18*(2), 150–171.

Farneti, F., & Guthrie, J. (2009). Sustainability reporting by Australian public sector organisations: Why they report. *Accounting Forum, 33*(2), 89–98.

Fedyk, A., Hodson, J., Khimich, N., & Fedyk, T. (2022). Is artificial intelligence improving the audit process? *Review of Accounting Studies, 27*(3), 938–985.

Fischer, D. G., & Rosenzweig, K. (1995). Attitudes of students and accounting practitioners concerning the ethical acceptability of earnings management. *Journal of Business Ethics, 14*, 433–444.

Fisher, I. E., Garnsey, M. R., & Hughes, M. E. (2016). Natural language processing in accounting, auditing and finance: A synthesis of the literature with a roadmap for future research. *Intelligent Systems in Accounting, Finance and Management, 23*(3), 157–214.

Fisher, D., & Lovell, A. (2009). *Business ethics and values: Individual, corporate and international perspectives.* Pearson Education.

Fleisch, E., Weinberger, M., & Wortmann, F. (2015). Business models and the Internet of Things. In *Interoperability and Open-Source Solutions for the Internet of Things: International Workshop, FP7 OpenIoT Project, Held in Conjunction with SoftCOM 2014*, Split, Croatia, September 18, 2014, Invited Papers (pp. 6–10). Springer International Publishing.

Flower, J. (2015). The international integrated reporting council: A story of failure. *Critical Perspectives on Accounting, 27*, 1–17.

Francis, R., & Armstrong, A. (2003). Ethics as a risk management strategy: The Australian experience. *Journal of Business Ethics, 45*, 375–385.

Francis, J. R., & Yu, M. D. (2009). Big 4 office size and audit quality. *The Accounting Review, 84*(5), 1521–1552.

Freeman, R. E., Harrison, J. S., Wicks, A. C., Parmar, B. L., & Colle, S. D. (2010). *Stakeholder theory: The state of the art.* Cambridge University Press.

Geijsbeek, J. B. (1914). *Ancient double-entry bookkeeping: Lucas Pacioli's treatise (A. D. 1494 – The earliest known writer on bookkeeping).* John B. Geijsbeek.

Gendron, Y., Cooper, D. J., & Townley, B. (2007). The construction of auditing expertise in measuring government performance. *Accounting, Organizations and Society, 32*(1–2), 101–129.

Gibson, C. B., & Birkinshaw, J. (2004). The antecedents, consequences, and mediating role of organizational ambidexterity. *Academy of Management Journal, 47*(2), 209–226.

Giudici, P. (2018). Fintech risk management: A research challenge for Artificial intelligence in finance. *Frontiers in AI, 1*, 1.

Glass, R. S., & Bonnici, J. (1997). An experiential approach for teaching business ethics. *Teaching Business Ethics, 1*(2), 183–195.

Graen, G. B., & Uhl-Bien, M. (1995). Relationship-based approach to leadership: Development of leader-member exchange (LMX) theory of leadership over 25 years: Applying a multi-level multi-domain perspective. *The Leadership Quarterly, 6*(2), 219–247.

Granlund, M., & Lukka, K. (2017). Investigating highly established research paradigms: Reviving contextuality in contingency theory based management accounting research. *Critical Perspectives on Accounting, 45*, 63–80.

Gray, R. (2002). The social accounting project and accounting organizations and society privileging engagement, imaginings, new accountings and pragmatism over critique? *Accounting, Organizations and Society, 27*(7), 687–708.

Gray, R., Adams, C., & Owen, D. (2014). *Accountability, social responsibility and sustainability: Accounting for society and the environment.* Pearson.

Gray, R., & Milne, M. (2018). Perhaps the Dodo should have accounted for human beings? Accounts of humanity and (its) extinction. *Accounting, Auditing & Accountability Journal, 31*(3), 826–848.

Gray, R., Owen, D., & Adams, C. (1996). *Accounting & accountability: Changes and challenges in corporate social and environmental reporting.* Prentice Hall.

Greenberg, J. (1994). Using socially fair treatment to promote acceptance of a work site smoking ban. *Journal of Applied Psychology, 79*(2), 288–297.

Greenfield, A. C., Norman, C. S., & Wier, B. (2008). The effect of ethical orientation and professional commitment on earnings management behavior. *Journal of Business Ethics, 83*, 419–434.

Grimaldi, M., Corvello, V., De Mauro, A., & Scarmozzino, E. (2017). A systematic literature review on intangible assets and open innovation. *Knowledge Management Research and Practice, 15*(1), 90–100.

Gubbi, J., Buyya, R., Marusic, S., & Palaniswami, M. (2013). Internet of Things: A vision, architectural elements, and future directions. *Future Generation Computer Systems, 29*(7), 1645–1660.

Gul, F. A., Srinidhi, B., & Ng, A. C. (2011). Does board gender diversity improve the informativeness of stock prices? *Journal of Accounting and Economics, 51*(3), 314–338.

Güngör, H. (2020). Creating value with AI: A multi-stakeholder perspective. *Journal of Creating Value, 6*(1), 72–85.

Hahn, R., & Kühnen, M. (2013). Determinants of sustainability reporting: A review of results, trends, theory, and opportunities in an expanding field of research. *Journal of Cleaner Production, 59*, 5–21.

Haller, A., & van Staden, C. (2014). The value added statement – An appropriate instrument for integrated reporting. *Accounting, Auditing & Accountability Journal, 27*(7), 1190–1216.

Han, H., Shiwakoti, R. K., Jarvis, R., Mordi, C., & Botchie, D. (2023). Accounting and auditing with blockchain technology and AI: A literature review. *International Journal of Accounting Information Systems, 48*.

Hanson, D., Hitt, M. A., Ireland, R. D., & Hoskisson, R. E. (2016). *Strategic management: Competitiveness and globalisation.* Cengage AU.

Hargreaves, T., Hielscher, S., Seyfang, G., & Smith, A. (2013). Grassroots innovations in community energy: The role of intermediaries in niche development. *Global Environmental Change, 23*(5), 868–880.

Hashem, I. A. T., Chang, V., Anuar, N. B., Adewole, K., Yaqoob, I., Gani, A., & Chiroma, H. (2016). The role of big data in smart city. *International Journal of Information Management, 36*(5), 748–758.

Healy, P. M., & Palepu, K. G. (2001). Information asymmetry, corporate disclosure, and the capital markets: A review of the empirical disclosure literature. *Journal of Accounting and Economics, 31*(1–3), 405–440.

Healy, P. M., & Palepu, K. G. (2003). The fall of Enron. *The Journal of Economic Perspectives, 17*(2), 3–26.

Hegel, G. W. F. (1807). *Phenomenology of spirit*. Oxford University Press.

Helfat, C. E., & Peteraf, M. A. (2003). The dynamic resource-based view: Capability lifecycles. *Strategic Management Journal, 24*(10), 997–1010.

Henderson, B. C., Peirson, G., & Herbohn, K. (2015). *Issues in financial accounting*. Pearson Higher Education AU.

Herath, S. K., & Richardson, G. D. (2018). In pursuit of a 'single source of truth': From threatened legitimacy to integrated reporting. *Journal of Business Ethics, 141*(1), 191–205.

Herzig, C., Viere, T., Schaltegger, S., & Burritt, R. (2012). *Environmental management accounting: Case studies of South-East Asian companies*. Routledge.

Hilson, G. (2002). Small-scale mining and its socio-economic impact in developing countries. *Natural Resources Forum, 26*(1), 3–13.

Hilson, G., & McQuilken, J. (2014). Four decades of support for artisanal and small-scale mining in sub-Saharan Africa: A critical review. *The Extractive Industries and Society, 1*(1), 104–118.

Hiltebeitel, K. M., & Jones, S. K. (1992). An assessment of ethics instruction in accounting education. *Journal of Business Ethics, 11*(1), 37–46.

Hinds, P. J., Carley, K. M., Krackhardt, D., & Wholey, D. (2002). Choosing work group members: Balancing similarity, competence, and familiarity. *Organizational Behavior and Human Decision Processes, 81*(2), 226–251.

Hinds, P. J., & Kiesler, S. (2002). *Distributed work: New research on working across distance using technology*. MIT Press.

Hockerts, K., & Moir, L. (2004). Communicating corporate responsibility to investors: The changing role of the investor relations function. *Journal of Business Ethics, 52*, 85–98.

Hodge, V. J., & Austin, J. (2004). A survey of outlier detection methodologies. *Artificial Intelligence Review, 22*(2), 85–126.

Hodge, V. J., O'Keefe, S., Weeks, M., & Moulds, A. (2014). Wireless sensor networks for condition monitoring in the railway industry: A survey. *IEEE Transactions on smart transportation systems, 16*(3), 1088–1106.

Hollands, R. G. (2020). Will the real smart city please stand up?: Smart, progressive or entrepreneurial? In *The Routledge companion to smart cities* (pp. 179–199). Routledge.

Hopper, T., & Major, M. (2007). Extending institutional analysis through theoretical triangulation: Regulation and activity-based costing in Portuguese telecommunications. *European Accounting Review, 16*(1), 59–97.

Hopwood, A. G. (2009). Accounting and the environment. *Accounting, Organizations and Society, 34*(3–4), 433–439.

Humphrey, C., Loft, A., & Woods, M. (2009). The global audit profession and the international financial architecture: Understanding regulatory relationships at a time of financial crisis. *Accounting, Organizations and Society, 34*(6–7), 810–825.

Huss, H. F., & Patterson, D. M. (1993). Ethics in accounting: Values education without indoctrination. *Journal of Business Ethics, 12*, 235–243.

Hysa, X., Kruja, A., Hagen, T., & Demaj, E. (2022). Smart-social business cities: The evolution, concepts, and determinants. In *Managing smart cities: Sustainability and resilience through effective management* (pp. 159–177). Springer International Publishing.

Issa, H., Sun, T., & Vasarhelyi, M. A. (2016). Research ideas for Artificial intelligence in auditing: The formalization of audit and workforce supplementation. *Journal of Emerging Technologies in Accounting*, *13*(2), 1–20.

Jackson, R. W., Wood, C. M., & Zboja, J. J. (2013). The dissolution of ethical decision-making in organizations: A comprehensive review and model. *Journal of Business Ethics*, *116*, 233–250.

Jansen, J. J., Van Den Bosch, F. A., & Volberda, H. W. (2009). Exploratory innovation, exploitative innovation, and ambidexterity: The impact of environmental and organizational antecedents. *Schmalenbach Business Review*, *57*(4), 351–363.

Janvrin, D. J., Raschke, R. L., & Dilla, W. N. (2014). Making sense of complex data using interactive data visualization. *Journal of Accounting Education*, *32*(4), 31–48.

Jennings, M. M. (2014). *Business: Its legal, ethical, and global environment*. Cengage Learning.

Jensen, M. C. (1993). The modern industrial revolution, exit, and the failure of internal control systems. *The Journal of Finance*, *48*(3), 831–880.

Jones, T. M. (1991). Ethical decision making by individuals in organizations: An issue-contingent model. *Academy of Management Review*, *16*(2), 366–395.

Jørgensen, B., & Messner, M. (2010). Accounting and strategising: A case study from new product development. *Accounting, Organizations and Society*, *35*(2), 184–204.

Kaptein, M. (2008a). Developing a measure of unethical behavior in the workplace: A stakeholder perspective. *Journal of Management*, *34*(5), 978–1008.

Kaptein, M. (2008b). Developing and testing a measure for the ethical culture of organizations: The corporate ethical virtues model. *Journal of Organizational Behavior*, *29*(7), 923–947.

Karpoff, J. M., Lee, D. S., & Martin, G. S. (2008). The cost to firms of cooking the books. *Journal of Financial and Quantitative Analysis*, *43*(3), 581–611.

Kiayias, A., Russell, A., David, B., & Oliynykov, R. (2017). Ouroboros: A provably secure proof-of-stake blockchain protocol. In *Annual International Cryptology Conference* (pp. 357–388). Springer.

Kiel, D., Müller, J. M., Arnold, C., & Voigt, K. I. (2017). Sustainable industrial value creation: Benefits and challenges of Industry 4.0. *International Journal of Innovation Management*, *21*(08), 1740015.

Kiljander, J., Ylisaukko-oja, A., Takalo-Mattila, J., Eteläperä, M., & Systä, K. (2014). Semantic interoperability architecture for pervasive computing and Internet of Things. *IEEE Access*, *2*, 856–873.

Kitchin, R. (2014). The real-time city? Big data and smart urbanism. *Geojournal*, *79*(1), 1–14.

Kitchin, R., & Dodge, M. (2011). *Code/space: Software and everyday life*. MIT Press.

Klettner, A., Clarke, T., & Boersma, M. (2014). The governance of corporate sustainability: Empirical insights into the development, leadership and implementation of responsible business strategy. *Journal of Business Ethics*, *122*(1), 145–165.

Knechel, W. R., & Willekens, M. (2006). The role of risk management and governance in determining audit demand. *Journal of Business Finance & Accounting*, *33*(9–10), 1344–1367.

Knechel, W. R., Krishnan, G. V., Pevzner, M., Shefchik, L. B., & Velury, U. K. (2013). Audit quality: Insights from the academic literature. *Auditing: A Journal of Practice & Theory, 32*(1), 385–421.

Knowles, M. S. (1984). *Andragogy in action.* Jossey-Bass.

Kokina, J., & Davenport, T. H. (2017). The emergence of AI: How automation is changing auditing. *Journal of Emerging Technologies in Accounting, 14*(1), 115–122.

Kokina, J., Mancha, R., & Pachamanova, D. (2017). Blockchain: Emergent industry adoption and implications for accounting. *Journal of Emerging Technologies in Accounting, 14*(2), 91–100.

Kolk, A. (2010). Trajectories of sustainability reporting by MNCs. *Journal of World Business, 45*(4), 367–374.

Koshizuka, N., & Sakamura, K. (2010). Ubiquitous ID: Standards for ubiquitous computing and the Internet of Things. *IEEE Pervasive Computing, 9*(4), 98–101.

Kotter, J. P. (1996). *Leading change.* Harvard Business School Press.

Kruja, A. (2020). Entrepreneurial orientation, synergy and firm performance in the agribusiness context: An emerging market economy perspective. *Central European Business Review, 9*(1), 56.

Kruja, A. D., Hysa, X., Duman, T., & Tafaj, A. (2019). Adoption of software as a service (SaaS) in small and medium-sized hotels in Tirana. *Enlightening Tourism. A Pathmaking Journal, 9*(2), 137–167.

Kshetri, N. (2018). Blockchain's roles in meeting key supply chain management objectives. *International Journal of Information Management, 39*, 80–89.

Kumar, A., & Ravi, V. (2007). Bankruptcy prediction in banks and firms via statistical and intelligent techniques – A review. *European Journal of Operational Research, 180*(1), 1–28.

Laine, M., Tregidga, H., & Unerman, J. (2021). *Sustainability accounting and accountability.* Routledge.

Lambert, C., & Sponem, S. (2012). Roles, authority and involvement of the management accounting function: A multiple case-study perspective. *European Accounting Review, 21*(3), 565–589.

Lambin, E. F., Meyfroidt, P., Rueda, X., Blackman, A., Börner, J., Cerutti, P. O., & Wunder, S. (2014). Effectiveness and synergies of policy instruments for land use governance in tropical regions. *Global Environmental Change, 28*, 129–140.

Langenderfer, H. Q., & Rockness, J. W. (1989). Integrating ethics into the accounting curriculum: Issues, problems, and solutions. *Issues in Accounting Education, 4*(1), 58–69.

Lardo, A., Corsi, K., Varma, A., & Mancini, D. (2022). Exploring blockchain in the accounting domain: A bibliometric analysis. *Accounting, Auditing & Accountability Journal, 35*(9), 204–233.

Larivière, B., Bowen, D., Andreassen, T. W., Kunz, W., Sirianni, N. J., Voss, C., & De Keyser, A. (2017). "Service Encounter 2.0": An investigation into the roles of technology, employees and customers. *Journal of Business Research, 79*, 238–246.

Lasi, H., Fettke, P., Kemper, H. G., Feld, T., & Hoffmann, M. (2014). Industry 4.0. *Business & Information Systems Engineering, 6*(4), 239–242.

Lavie, D., Stettner, U., & Tushman, M. L. (2010). Exploration and exploitation within and across organizations. *The Academy of Management Annals, 4*(1), 109–155.

Lawrence, J., Rasche, A., & Kenny, K. (2018). Sustainability as opportunity: Unilever's sustainable living plan. In *Managing sustainable business: An executive education case and textbook* (pp. 435–455). Springer Netherlands.

Le Billon, P. (2008). Diamond wars? Conflict diamonds and geographies of resource wars. *Annals of the Association of American Geographers, 98*(2), 345–372.

Lee, J., Bagheri, B., & Kao, H. A. (2014). A cyber-physical systems architecture for industry 4.0-based manufacturing systems. *Manufacturing Letters, 3*, 18–23.

Lee, C. S., & Tajudeen, F. P. (2020). Usage and impact of artificial intelligence on accounting: Evidence from Malaysian organisations. *Asian Journal of Business and Accounting, 13*(1).

Lennox, C. (2005). Audit quality and executive officers' affiliations with CPA firms. *Journal of Accounting and Economics, 39*(2), 201–231.

Leoni, G., Bergamaschi, F., & Maione, G. (2021). Artificial intelligence and local governments: The case of strategic performance management systems and accountability. In A. Visvizi & M. Bodziany (Eds.), *Artificial intelligence and its context: Security, business and governance* (pp. 1613–5113). Springer. ISSN: 1613-5113. E-ISSN: 2363-9466. ISBN: 978-3-030-88971-5 ISBN (e-Book): 978-3-030-88972-2. https://doi.org/10.1007/978-3-030-88972-2

Leuz, C., & Wysocki, P. D. (2016). The economics of disclosure and financial reporting regulation: Evidence and suggestions for future research. *Journal of Accounting Research, 54*(2), 525–622.

Li, F., Nucciarelli, A., Roden, S., & Graham, G. (2016). How smart cities transform operations models: A new research agenda for operations management in the digital economy. *Production Planning & Control, 27*(6), 514–528.

Lipton, M., & Lorsch, J. W. (1992). A modest proposal for improved corporate governance. *The Business Lawyer, 48*(1), 59–77.

Liu, M., Wu, K., & Xu, J. J. (2019). How will blockchain technology impact auditing and accounting: Permissionless versus permissioned blockchain. *Current Issues in auditing, 13*(2), A19–A29.

Loeb, S. E. (1991). The evaluation of "outcomes" of accounting ethics education. *Journal of Business Ethics, 10*(2), 77–84.

Loia, V., Maione, G., Tommasetti, A., Torre, C., Troisi, O., & Botti, A. (2016). Toward smart value co-education. In *Smart Education and e-Learning 2016* (pp. 61–71). Springer International Publishing.

Loughran, T., & McDonald, B. (2016). Textual analysis in accounting and finance: A survey. *Journal of Accounting Research, 54*(4), 1187–1230.

Lozano, R. (2013). Are companies planning their organisational changes for corporate sustainability? An analysis of three case studies on resistance to change and their strategies to overcome it. *Corporate Social Responsibility and Environmental Management, 20*(5), 275–295.

Lozano, R., & Huisingh, D. (2011). Inter-linking issues and dimensions in sustainability reporting. *Journal of Cleaner Production, 19*(2–3), 99–107.

Lubin, D. A., & Esty, D. C. (2010). The sustainability imperative. *Harvard Business Review, 88*(5), 42–50.

Luo, X., & Bhattacharya, C. B. (2006). Corporate social responsibility, customer satisfaction, and market value. *Journal of Marketing, 70*(4), 1–18.

Lytras, M. D., Chui, K. T., & Visvizi, A. (2019). Data analytics in smart healthcare: The recent developments and beyond. *Applied Sciences, 9*(14), 2812.

Lytras, M. D., & Visvizi, A. (2018). Who uses smart city services and what to make of it: Toward interdisciplinary smart cities research. *Sustainability*, *10*(6), 1998.

Lytras, M. D., & Visvizi, A. (2021). Artificial intelligence and cognitive computing: Methods, technologies, systems, applications and policy making. *Sustainability*, *13*(7), 3598.

Maione, G. (2023). An energy company's journey toward standardized sustainability reporting: Addressing governance challenges. *Transforming Government: People, Process and Policy*, *17*(3), 356–371. https://doi.org/10.1108/TG-05-2023-0062

Maione, G., Cuccurullo, C., & Tommasetti, A. (2023a). An algorithmic historiography of biodiversity accounting literature. *Accounting, Auditing & Accountability Journal*, *36*(6), 1665–1694. https://doi.org/10.1108/AAAJ-06-2022-5883

Maione, G., Cuccurullo, C., & Tommasetti, A. (2023b). Biodiversity accounting: A bibliometric analysis for comprehensive literature mapping. *Sustainability Accounting, Management and Policy Journal*. https://doi.org/10.1108/SAMPJ-04-2022-0214

Maione, G., & Leoni, G. (2021). Artificial Intelligence and the public sector: The case of accounting. In A. Visvizi & M. Bodziany (Eds.), *Artificial intelligence and its context: Security, business and governance*. Springer. ISSN: 1613-5113. E-ISSN: 2363-9466. ISBN: 978-3-030-88971-5 ISBN (e-Book): 978-3-030-88972-2. https://doi.org/10.1007/978-3-030-88972-2

Maione, G., Sorrentino, D., & Kruja, A. D. (2022). Open data for accountability at times of exception: An exploratory analysis during the COVID-19 pandemic. *Transforming Government: People, Process and Policy*, *16*(2), 231–243. https://doi.org/10.1108/TG-06-2021-0093

Malik, R., Visvizi, A., Troisi, O., & Grimaldi, M. (2022). Smart services in smart cities: Insights from science mapping analysis. *Sustainability*, *14*(11), 6506.

Malsch, B., & Gendron, Y. (2013). Re-theorizing change: Institutional experimentation and the struggle for domination in the field of public accounting. *Journal of Management Studies*, *50*(5), 870–899.

Malviya, B. K., & Lal, P. (2021). The changing face of accounting: Prospects and issues in the application of AI. *International Journal of Accounting, Business and Finance*, *1*(1), 1–7.

Manski, S. (2017). Building the blockchain world: Technological commonwealth or just more of the same? *Strategic Change*, *26*(5), 511–522.

Matten, D., & Moon, J. (2004). Corporate social responsibility. *Journal of Business Ethics*, *54*, 323–337.

Mattern, F., & Floerkemeier, C. (2010). From the internet of computers to the Internet of Things. In K. Sachs, I. Petrov, & P. Guerrero (Eds.), *From active data management to event-based systems and more*. Springer.

Mattessich, R. (2003). Accounting research and researchers of the nineteenth century and the beginning of the twentieth century: An international survey of authors, ideas and publications. *Accounting Business and Financial History*, *13*(2), 125–170.

Maurer, R. (2010). *Beyond the wall of resistance: Why 70% of all changes still fail-and what you can do about it*. Bard Press.

Mazzara, L., Maione, G., & Leoni, G. (2023). Performance measurement and management systems in local government networks: Stimulating resilience through dynamic capabilities. In A. Visvizi, O. Troisi & M. Grimaldi (Eds.),

Proceeding of Research & Innovation Forum 2022 (RII Forum) – Rupture, Resilience and Recovery in the Post-Covid World, Atene, Grecia, 20–22 April 2022 (pp. 539–546). Springer. ISBN: 978-3-031-19559-4. https://doi.org/10.1007/978-3-031-19560-0

McPhail, K., & Walters, D. (2009). *Accounting and business ethics: An introduction.* Routledge.

Meske, C., Bunde, E., Schneider, J., & Gersch, M. (2022). Explainable AI: Objectives, stakeholders, and future research opportunities. *Information Systems Management, 39*(1), 53–63.

Meyer, J. P., & Herscovitch, L. (2001). Commitment in the workplace: Toward a general model. *Human Resource Management Review, 11*(3), 299–326.

Miceli, M. P., Near, J. P., & Dworkin, T. M. (2008). *Whistle-blowing in organizations.* Psychology Press.

Miers, I., Garman, C., Green, M., & Rubin, A. D. (2013, May). Zerocoin: Anonymous distributed e-cash from bitcoin. In *2013 IEEE Symposium on Security and Privacy* (pp. 397–411). IEEE.

Milne, M. J., & Gray, R. (2013). W(h)ither ecology? The triple bottom line, the global reporting initiative, and corporate sustainability reporting. *Journal of Business Ethics, 118*(1), 13–29.

Mintz, S., & Morris, R. E. (2022). *Ethical obligations and decision making in accounting.* McGraw-Hill Higher Education.

Mirakhor, A., & Askari, H. (2010). *Islam and the path to human and economic development.* Palgrave Macmillan.

Mitchell, R. K., Agle, B. R., & Wood, D. J. (1997). Toward a theory of stakeholder identification and salience: Defining the principle of who and what really counts. *Academy of Management Review, 22*(4), 853–886.

Mobley, R. K. (2002). *An introduction to predictive maintenance.* Elsevier.

Moodaley, W., & Telukdarie, A. (2023). Greenwashing, sustainability reporting, and AI: A systematic literature review. *Sustainability, 15*(2), 1481.

Moore, G., Roper, I., & Cheney, G. (2006). The future of corporate social responsibility. In S. K. May, G. Cheney, & J. Roper (Eds.), (2007). *The debate over corporate social responsibility* (pp. 25–39). Oxford University Press.

Morrison, R. (2015). *Data-driven organization design: Sustaining the competitive edge through organizational analytics.* Kogan Page Publishers.

Morrison, S. (2016). *Blockchain and smart contract automation: How smart contracts automate digital business.* Blockchain Research Institute.

Mougayar, W. (2016). *The business blockchain: Promise, practice, and application of the next Internet technology.* Wiley.

Mussari, R., Tommasetti, A., Maione, G., & Sorrentino, D. (2020). L'etica contabile: un'analisi della letteratura tra passato, presente e futuro. In *Dalla crisi allo sviluppo sostenibile: principi e soluzioni nella prospettiva economico-aziendale* (pp. 1–21). Franco Angeli.

Nakamoto, S. (2008). Bitcoin: A peer-to-peer electronic cash system. *Decentralized Business Review*, 1–9.

Nakasumi, M. (2017). Information sharing for supply chain management based on block chain technology. In *2017 14th IEEE Annual Consumer Communications & Networking Conference (CCNC)* (pp. 1–5). IEEE.

Narayanan, A., Bonneau, J., Felten, E., Miller, A., & Goldfeder, S. (2016). *Bitcoin and cryptocurrency technologies: A comprehensive introduction.* Princeton University Press.

Nelson, M. W. (2009). A model and literature review of professional skepticism in auditing. *Auditing: A Journal of Practice & Theory, 28*(2), 1–34.

Nelson, R. R., & Winter, S. G. (1985). *An evolutionary theory of economic change.* Belknap Press of Harvard University Press.

Nembhard, I. M., & Edmondson, A. C. (2006). Making it safe: The effects of leader inclusiveness and professional status on psychological safety and improvement efforts in health care teams. *Journal of Organizational Behavior, 27*(7), 941–966.

Nishant, R., Kennedy, M., & Corbett, J. (2020). Artificial intelligence for sustainability: Challenges, opportunities, and a research agenda. *International Journal of Information Management, 53*, 102104.

Nobes, C. (2011). IFRS practices and the persistence of accounting system classification. *Abacus, 47*(3), 267–283.

Nobes, C., & Parker, R. H. (2008). *Comparative international accounting.* Pearson Higher Education.

Nobes, C., Parker, R. B., & Parker, R. H. (2008). *Comparative international accounting.* Pearson Education.

O'Dwyer, B., & Owen, D. (2005). Assurance statement practice in environmental, social, and sustainability reporting: A critical evaluation. *The British Accounting Review, 37*(2), 205–229.

O'Leary, C. (2009). An empirical analysis of the positive impact of ethics teaching on accounting students. *Accounting Education, 18*(4–5), 505–520.

O'Reilly, C. A., & Tushman, M. L. (2004). The ambidextrous organization. *Harvard Business Review, 82*(4), 74–83.

Otley, D. (2016). The contingency theory of management accounting and control: 1980–2014. *Management Accounting Research, 31*, 45–62.

Owen, D. (2005). CSR after Enron: A role for the academic accounting profession? *European Accounting Review, 14*(2), 395–404.

Pang, B., & Lee, L. (2008). Opinion mining and sentiment analysis. *Foundations and Trends in Information Retrieval, 2*(1–2), 1–135.

Pantano, E., & Corvello, V. (2014). Tourists' acceptance of advanced technology-based innovations for promoting arts and culture. *International Journal of Technology Management, 64*(1), 3–16.

Parker, L. D. (1994). Professional accounting body ethics: In search of the private interest. *Accounting, Organizations and Society, 19*(6), 507–525.

Parker, S. K., & Axtell, C. M. (2001). Seeing another viewpoint: Antecedents and outcomes of employee perspective taking. *Academy of Management Journal, 44*(6), 1085–1100.

Penman, S. H. (2007). Financial reporting quality: Is fair value a plus or a minus? *Accounting and Business Research, 37*(1), 33–44.

Penman, S. H. (2013). *Financial statement analysis and security valuation.* McGraw-Hill Education.

Pereira, A. C., & Romero, F. (2017). A review of the meanings and the implications of the Industry 4.0 concept. *Procedia Manufacturing, 13*, 1206–1214.

Perera, C., Qin, Y., Estrella, J. C., Reiff-Marganiec, S., & Vasilakos, A. V. (2017). Fog computing for sustainable smart cities: A survey. *ACM Computing Surveys*, *50*(3), 1–43.

Perri, C., Giglio, C., & Corvello, V. (2020). Smart users for smart technologies: Investigating the intention to adopt smart energy consumption behaviors. *Technological Forecasting and Social Change*, *155*, 119991.

Pfeffer, J. (2010). Building sustainable organizations: The human factor. *Academy of Management Perspectives*, *24*(1), 34–45.

Pimentel, E., & Boulianne, E. (2020). Blockchain in accounting research and practice: Current trends and future opportunities. *Accounting Perspectives*, *19*(4), 325–361.

Polese, F., Ciasullo, M. V., Troisi, O., & Maione, G. (2019). Sustainability in footwear industry: A big data analysis. *Sinergie Italian Journal of Management*, *37*(1), 149–170.

Polese, F., Tommasetti, A., Vesci, M., Carrubbo, L., & Troisi, O. (2016). Decision-making in smart service systems: A viable systems approach contribution to service science advances. In *Exploring Services Science: 7th International Conference, IESS 2016*, May 25–27, 2016 (Vol. 7, pp. 3–14). Springer International Publishing.

Polese, F., Troisi, O., Grimaldi, M., & Loia, F. (2021). Reinterpreting governance in smart cities: An ecosystem-based view. In *Smart cities and the un SDGs* (pp. 71–89). Elsevier.

Polikar, R. (2006). Ensemble based systems in decision making. *IEEE Circuits and Systems Magazine*, *6*(3), 21–45.

Ponemon, L. A. (1992). Ethical reasoning and selection-socialization in accounting. *Accounting, Organizations and Society*, *17*(3–4), 239–258.

Previts, G. J., & Merino, B. D. (1979). *A history of accounting in America: An historical interpretation of the cultural significance of accounting*. The Blackburn Press.

Pries, K. H., & Dunnigan, R. (2015). *Big Data analytics: A practical guide for managers*. CRC Press.

Rajgopal, S. (1999). Early evidence on the informativeness of the SEC's market risk disclosures: The case of commodity price risk exposure of oil and gas producers. *The Accounting Review*, *74*(3), 251–280.

Ramanna, K. (2008). The implications of unverifiable fair-value accounting: Evidence from the political economy of goodwill accounting. *Journal of Accounting and Economics*, *45*(2–3), 253–281.

Rejeb, A., Keogh, J. G., & Treiblmaier, H. (2019). Leveraging the Internet of Things and blockchain technology in supply chain management. *Future Internet*, *11*(7), 161.

Rezaee, Z. (2005). Causes, consequences, and deterence of financial statement fraud. *Critical Perspectives on Accounting*, *16*(3), 277–298.

Rimmel, G., & Jonäll, K. (2013). Biodiversity reporting in Sweden: Corporate disclosure and preparers' views. *Accounting, Auditing & Accountability Journal*, *26*(5), 746–778.

Roberts, R. W., & Bobek, D. D. (2004). The politics of tax accounting in the United States: Evidence from the Taxpayer Relief Act of 1997. *Accounting, Organizations and Society*, *29*(5–6), 565–590.

Roca, L. C., & Searcy, C. (2012). An analysis of indicators disclosed in corporate sustainability reports. *Journal of Cleaner Production, 20*(1), 103–118.

Rockström, J., Gaffney, O., Rogelj, J., Meinshausen, M., Nakicenovic, N., & Schellnhuber, H. J. (2017). A roadmap for rapid decarbonization. *Science, 355*(6331), 1269–1271.

Rogan, M., & Mors, M. L. (2014). A network perspective on individual-level ambidexterity in organizations. *Organization Science, 25*(6), 1860–1877.

Roman, R., Zhou, J., & Lopez, J. (2013). On the features and challenges of security and privacy in distributed Internet of Things. *Computer Networks, 57*(10), 2266–2279.

Romano, R. (2005). The Sarbanes-Oxley Act and the making of quack corporate governance. *Yale LJ, 114*, 1521.

Rosen, R., Von Wichert, G., Lo, G., & Bettenhausen, K. D. (2015). About the importance of autonomy and digital twins for the future of manufacturing. *IFAC-PapersOnLine, 48*(3), 567–572.

Russell, S. J., & Norvig, P. (2016). *Artificial intelligence: A modern approach.* Pearson.

Rüßmann, M., Lorenz, M., Gerbert, P., Waldner, M., Justus, J., Engel, P., & Harnisch, M. (2015). Industry 4.0: The future of productivity and growth in manufacturing industries. *Boston Consulting Group, 9*(1), 54–89.

Sadeghi, M., Mahmoudi, A., Deng, X., & Luo, X. (2023). Prioritizing requirements for implementing blockchain technology in construction supply chain based on circular economy: Fuzzy Ordinal Priority Approach. *International Journal of Environmental Science and Technology, 20*(5), 4991–5012.

Sangster, A. (2016). The genesis of double entry bookkeeping. *The Accounting Review, 91*(1), 299–315.

Scarmozzino, E., Corvello, V., & Grimaldi, M. (2017). Entrepreneurial learning through online social networking in high-tech startups. *International Journal of Entrepreneurial Behavior & Research, 23*(3), 406–425.

Schaltegger, S., & Wagner, M. (2006). Integrative management of sustainability performance, measurement and reporting. *International Journal of Accounting, Auditing and Performance Evaluation, 3*(1), 1–19.

Schein, E. H. (2010). *Organizational culture and leadership.* John Wiley & Sons.

Schmidt, R., Möhring, M., Härting, R. C., Reichstein, C., Neumaier, P., & Jozinović, P. (2015). Industry 4.0 – Potentials for creating smart products: Empirical research results. In *International conference on business information systems* (pp. 16–27). Springer.

Schmitz, J., & Leoni, G. (2019). Accounting and auditing at the time of blockchain technology: A research agenda. *Australian Accounting Review, 29*(2), 331–342.

Searcy, C. (2012). Corporate sustainability performance measurement systems: A review and research agenda. *Journal of Business Ethics, 107*(3), 239–253.

Sezer, O. B., & Ozbayoglu, A. M. (2018). Algorithmic financial trading with deep convolutional neural networks: Time series to image conversion approach. *Applied Soft Computing, 70*, 525–538.

Shafer, W. E., Morris, R. E., & Ketchand, A. A. (2001). Effects of personal values on auditors' ethical decisions. *Accounting, Auditing & Accountability Journal, 14*(3), 254–277.

Sicari, S., Rizzardi, A., Grieco, L. A., & Coen-Porisini, A. (2015). Security, privacy and trust in Internet of Things: The road ahead. *Computer Networks, 76*, 146–164.

Sikka, P. (2015a). No accounting for tax avoidance. *The Political Quarterly*, *86*(3), 427–433.

Sikka, P. (2015b). The hand of accounting and accountancy firms in deepening income and wealth inequalities and the economic crisis: Some evidence. *Critical Perspectives on Accounting*, *30*, 46–62.

Simnett, R., & Huggins, A. L. (2015). Integrated reporting and assurance: Where can research add value? *Sustainability Accounting, Management and Policy Journal*, *6*(1), 29–53.

Simnett, R., Vanstraelen, A., & Chua, W. F. (2009). Assurance on sustainability reports: An international comparison. *The Accounting Review*, *91*(3), 937–967.

Simsek, Z., Heavey, C., Veiga, J. F., & Souder, D. (2009). A typology for aligning organizational ambidexterity's conceptualizations, antecedents, and outcomes. *Journal of Management Studies*, *46*(5), 864–894.

Sirmon, D. G., Hitt, M. A., & Ireland, R. D. (2007). Managing firm resources in dynamic environments to create value: Looking inside the black box. *Academy of Management Review*, *32*(1), 273–292.

Smith, W. K., & Tushman, M. L. (2005). Managing strategic contradictions: A top management model for managing innovation streams. *Organization Science*, *16*(5), 522–536.

Soll, J. (2014). *The reckoning: Financial accountability and the making and breaking of nations*. Basic Books.

Solomons, D. (1991). Accounting and social change: A neutralist view. *Accounting, Organizations and Society*, *16*(3), 287–295.

Spanò, R., Massaro, M., Ferri, L., Dumay, J., & Schmitz, J. (2022). Blockchain in accounting, accountability and assurance: An overview. *Accounting, Auditing & Accountability Journal*, *35*(7), 1493–1506.

Spender, J. C., Corvello, V., Grimaldi, M., & Rippa, P. (2017). Startups and open innovation: A review of the literature. *European Journal of Innovation Management*, *20*(1), 4–30.

Srinivasan, R., & González, B. S. M. (2022). The role of empathy for artificial intelligence accountability. *Journal of Responsible Technology*, *9*, 100021.

Stiglitz, J. E. (2010). *Freefall: America, free markets, and the sinking of the world economy*. WW Norton & Company.

Sun, T. (2019). Applying deep learning to audit procedures: An illustrative framework. *Accounting Horizons*, *33*(3), 89–109.

Sun, J., Yan, J., & Zhang, K. Z. (2016). Blockchain-based sharing services: What blockchain technology can contribute to smart cities. *Financial Innovation*, *2*(1), 1–9.

Susskind, L., & Cruikshank, J. (1987). *Breaking the impasse: Consensual approaches to resolving public disputes*. Basic Books.

Susskind, R., & Susskind, D. (2015). *The future of the professions: How technology will transform the work of human experts*. Oxford University Press.

Svanberg, J., & Öhman, P. (2013). Auditors' time pressure: Does ethical culture support audit quality? *Managerial Auditing Journal*, *30*(7), 572–591.

Sweeney, B., & Costello, F. (2009). Moral intensity and ethical decision-making: An empirical examination of undergraduate accounting and business students. *Accounting Education*, *18*(1), 75–97.

Tapscott, D., & Tapscott, A. (2016). *Blockchain revolution: How the technology behind bitcoin is changing money, business, and the world*. Penguin.

Teece, D. J. (2007). Explicating dynamic capabilities: The nature and microfoundations of (sustainable) enterprise performance. *Strategic Management Journal, 28*(13), 1319–1350.

Teece, D. J., Pisano, G., & Shuen, A. (1997). Dynamic capabilities and strategic management. *Strategic Management Journal, 18*(7), 509–533.

Teh, D., & Rana, T. (2023). The use of Internet of Things, Big Data analytics and artificial intelligence for attaining UN's SDGs. In *Handbook of big data and analytics in accounting and auditing* (pp. 235–253). Springer Nature.

Tekathen, M., & Dechow, N. (2013). Enterprise risk management and continuous re-alignment in the pursuit of accountability: A German case. *Management Accounting Research, 24*(2), 100–121.

Tetlock, P. C. (2007). Giving content to investor sentiment: The role of media in the stock market. *The Journal of Finance, 62*(3), 1139–1168.

Tommasetti, A., Del Bene, L., Maione, G., & Leoni, G. (2020). Environmental reporting, accountability and governance of local governments: An Italian multiple case study. *African Journal of Business Management, 14*(8), 229–242. https://doi.org/10.5897/AJBM2020.9027

Tommasetti, A., Maione, G., Lentini, P., & Bignardi, A. (2023). Environmental accounting in the public sector: A systematic literature review. *International Journal of Business Environment, 14*(2), 164–182. https://doi.org/10.1504/IJBE.2022.10049134

Tommasetti, A., Mazzara, L., Leoni, G., & Maione, G. (2021). Local governments as service ecosystems: Technology for accountability during the pandemic. In *Proceedings of the 24th Excellence in Services International Conference (EISIC)*, Salerno, 02–03 September 2021. ISBN: 979-12-200-9171-8.

Tommasetti, A., Mussari, R., Maione, G., & Sorrentino, D. (2020). Sustainability accounting and reporting in the public sector: Towards public value co-creation? *Sustainability, 12*(5), 1909–1928. https://doi.org/10.3390/su12051909

Treem, J. W., & Leonardi, P. M. (2013). Social media use in organizations: Exploring the affordances of visibility, editability, persistence, and association. *Annals of the International Communication Association, 36*(1), 143–189.

Treviño, L. K., Butterfield, K. D., & McCabe, D. L. (1998). The ethical context in organizations: Influences on employee attitudes and behaviors. *Business Ethics Quarterly, 8*(3), 447–476.

Treviño, L. K., Hartman, L. P., & Brown, M. (2000). Moral person and moral manager: How executives develop a reputation for ethical leadership. *California Management Review, 42*(4), 128–142.

Treviño, L. K., Nieuwenboer, N. A. D., Kreiner, G. E., & Bishop, D. G. (2014). Legitimating the legitimate: A grounded theory study of legitimacy work among ethics and compliance officers. *Organizational Behavior and Human Decision Processes, 123*(2), 186–205.

Treviño, L. K., Weaver, G. R., & Reynolds, S. J. (2006). Behavioral ethics in organizations: A review. *Journal of Management, 32*(6), 951–990.

Troisi, O., D'Arco, M., Loia, F., & Maione, G. (2018). Big data management: The case of Mulino Bianco's engagement platform for value co-creation. *International Journal of Engineering Business Management, 10*. https://doi.org/10.1177/1847979018767776

Troisi, O., Grimaldi, M., Loia, F., & Maione, G. (2018). Big data and sentiment analysis to highlight decision behaviours: A case study for student population. *Behaviour & Information Technology, 37*(10–11), 1111–1128.

Troisi, O., Grimaldi, M., & Monda, A. (2019). Managing smart service ecosystems through technology: How ICTs enable value cocreation. *Tourism Analysis, 24*(3), 377–393.

Troisi, O., Santovito, S., Carrubbo, L., & Sarno, D. (2019). Evaluating festival attributes adopting SD logic: The mediating role of visitor experience and visitor satisfaction. *Marketing Theory, 19*(1), 85–102.

Troisi, O., Sarno, D., Maione, G., & Loia, F. (2019). Service science management engineering and design (SSMED): A semiautomatic literature review. *Journal of Marketing Management, 35*(11–12), 1015–1046.

Tsui, J. S. (1996). Auditors' ethical reasoning: Some audit conflict and cross cultural evidence. *The International Journal of Accounting, 31*(1), 121–133.

Tushman, M. L., & O'Reilly, C. A. (1996). Ambidextrous organizations: Managing evolutionary and revolutionary change. *California Management Review, 38*(4), 8–29.

Uc, M., & Shehu, D. (2017). The attitudes of internal auditors to internal audit practice in post-communist countries-case of Albania. *Accounting and Finance Research, 6*(3), 1–88.

Unerman, J., Bebbington, J., & O'Dwyer, B. (2021). In M. Laine, H. Tregidga, & J. Unerman (Eds.), *Sustainability accounting and accountability* (pp. 3–14). Routledge.

Unerman, J., & Bennett, M. (2004). Increased stakeholder dialogue and the internet: Towards greater corporate accountability or reinforcing capitalist hegemony? *Accounting, Organizations and Society, 29*(7), 685–707.

Unerman, J., & Zappettini, F. (2014). Incorporating materiality considerations into analyses of absence from sustainability reporting. *Social and Environmental Accountability Journal, 34*(3), 172–186.

Unilever. (2012). *Unilever annual report and accounts 2012* [Report]. https://assets.unilever.com/files/92ui5egz/production/838d89bcbb4b3aac60cf48e31db0374911e0bf6b.pdf/ir-unilever-ar12.pdf

Unilever. (2013). *Unilever annual report and accounts 2013* [Report]. https://assets.unilever.com/files/92ui5egz/production/57d96b7700473ad2f70167a24fdfd425ee960b92.pdf/unilever-ar13.pdf

Unilever. (2014). *Unilever annual report and accounts 2014* [Report]. https://assets.unilever.com/files/92ui5egz/production/bff0a3b0727b0222fe5226f1b052639708cab2c3.pdf/ir-unilever-ar14.pdf

Unilever. (2015). *Unilever annual report and accounts 2015* [Report]. https://www.unilever-northlatam.com/files/origin/4aafe51457f6da33260362af11cbde90078a6550.pdf/annual-reports-and-accounts-2015.pdf

Unilever. (2016). *Unilever annual report and accounts 2016* [Report]. https://www.unilever.com/files/92ui5egz/production/813f7bacbbeac5e39ee1ed77dc4fde161e2e0055.pdf

Unilever. (2017). *Unilever annual report and accounts 2017* [Report]. https://assets.unilever.com/files/92ui5egz/production/6be0d0dbe8c5088374b7f3ff903ef4995a1a6a62.pdf/unilever-annual-report-and-accounts-2017.pdf

Unilever. (2018). *Unilever annual report and accounts 2018* [Report]. https://assets.unilever.com/files/92ui5egz/production/9fbb2cb4402c390d78734e74baa5360 3223abd8c.pdf/unilever-annual-report-and-accounts-2018.pdf

Unilever. (2019). *Unilever annual report and accounts 2019* [Report]. https://assets.unilever.com/files/92ui5egz/production/1e37dec387a6647bd6bd1c8d1bc8a8 6cd0135ed7.pdf/unilever-annual-report-and-accounts-2019.pdf

Unilever. (2020). *Unilever annual report and accounts 2020* [Report]. https://www.unilever.com/files/92ui5egz/production/372ab0178e9555aa5010f15aed8295af 77149fe3.pdf

Unilever. (2021). *Unilever annual report and accounts 2021* [Report]. https://www.unilever.com/files/92ui5egz/production/75f31d18a2219004f4afe03e37ccd2a3b 383472f.pdf

Unilever. (2022). *Unilever Annual Report and Accounts 2022* [Report]. https://www.unilever.co.uk/files/92ui5egz/production/257f12db9c95ffa2ed12d6f2e2b3ff67 db49fd60.pdf

Unilever. (2023). Unilever press releases [Media and Press Releases]. https://www.unilever.com/news/press-and-media/press-releases/?q=artificial+intelligence

van Deursen, A. J., & Mossberger, K. (2018). Any thing for anyone? A new digital divide in internet-of-things skills. *Policy & Internet, 10*(2), 122–140.

van Doorn, J., Mende, M., Noble, S. M., Hulland, J., Ostrom, A. L., Grewal, D., & Petersen, J. A. (2017). Domo Arigato Mr. Roboto: Emergence of automated social presence in organizational frontlines and customers' service experiences. *Journal of Service Research, 20*(1), 43–58.

Van Dyne, L., Ang, S., & Botero, I. C. (2003). Conceptualizing employee silence and employee voice as multidimensional constructs. *Journal of Management Studies, 40*(6), 1359–1392.

Vasarhelyi, M. A., Kogan, A., & Tuttle, B. M. (2015). Big data in accounting: An overview. *Accounting Horizons, 29*(2), 381–396.

Velte, P., & Stawinoga, M. (2017). Integrated reporting: The current state of empirical research, limitations and future research implications. *Journal of Management Control, 28*, 275–320.

Verschoor, C. C. (1998). A study of the link between a corporation's financial performance and its commitment to ethics. *Journal of Business Ethics, 17*(13), 1509–1516.

Visvizi, A., Lytras, M. D., Damiani, E., & Mathkour, H. (2018). Policy making for smart cities: Innovation and social inclusive economic growth for sustainability. *Journal of Science and Technology Policy Management, 9*(2), 126–133.

Visvizi, A., Lytras, M. D., & Sarirete, A. (2019). Emerging technologies and higher education: Management and administration in focus. In *Management and administration of higher education institutions at times of change* (pp. 1–11). Emerald Publishing Limited.

Visvizi, A., & Troisi, O. (Eds.). (2022). *Managing smart cities: Sustainability and resilience through effective management*. Springer Nature.

Voss, C., & Hsuan, J. (2009). Service architecture and modularity. *Decision Sciences, 40*(3), 541–569.

Watts, R. L., & Zimmerman, J. L. (1986). *Positive accounting theory*. Prentice-Hall.

Weber, R. H. (2010). Internet of Things – New security and privacy challenges. *Computer Law & Security Report, 26*(1), 23–30.

Weick, K. E., Sutcliffe, K. M., & Obstfeld, D. (2005). Organizing and the process of sensemaking. *Organization Science, 16*(4), 409–421.

Womack, J. P., Jones, D. T., & Roos, D. (1990). *The machine that changed the world*. Rawson Associates.

Yamey, B. S. (1949). Scientific bookkeeping and the rise of capitalism. *The Economic History Review, 1*(2–3), 99–113.

Yermack, D. (1996). Higher market valuation of companies with a small board of directors. *Journal of Financial Economics, 40*(2), 185–211.

Zamani, M., Movahedi, M., & Raykova, M. (2018). Rapidchain: Scaling blockchain via full sharding. In *Proceedings of the 2018 ACM SIGSAC Conference on Computer and Communications Security* (pp. 931–948). https://doi.org/10.1145/3243734.3243853

Zanella, A., Bui, N., Castellani, A., Vangelista, L., & Zorzi, M. (2014). Internet of Things for smart cities. *IEEE Internet of Things Journal, 1*(1), 22–32.

Zeff, S. A. (2015). *Forging accounting principles in five countries: A history and an analysis of trends*. Routledge.

Zetzsche, D. A., Buckley, R. P., Arner, D. W., & Föhr, L. (2018). *The ICO gold rush: It's a scam, it's a bubble, it's a super challenge for regulators*. University of Luxembourg Law Working Paper No. 11/2017.

Zhang, Z., Gu, Y., Jiang, L., Yu, W., & Dai, J. (2023). Internet of Things and blockchain-based smart contracts: Enabling continuous risk monitoring and assessment in peer-to-peer lending. *Journal of Emerging Technologies in Accounting*, 1–14.

Zhang, C., Zhu, W., Dai, J., Wu, Y., & Chen, X. (2023). Ethical impact of artificial intelligence in managerial accounting. *International Journal of Accounting Information Systems, 49*, 100619.

Zhao, J. L., Fan, S., & Yan, J. (2016). Overview of business innovations and research opportunities in blockchain and introduction to the special issue. *Financial Innovation, 2*(1), 1–7.

Zhong, R. Y., Xu, X., Klotz, E., & Newman, S. T. (2017). Smart manufacturing in the context of Industry 4.0: A review. *Engineering, 3*(5), 616–630.

Zhou, K., Liu, T., & Zhou, L. (2015). Industry 4.0: Towards future industrial opportunities and challenges. In *2015 12th International Conference on Fuzzy Systems and Knowledge Discovery (FSKD)* (pp. 2147–2152). IEEE.

Zimnisky, P. (2016). The state of global rough diamond supply 2014. *Rough Diamond Review, 7*(2), 8–13.

Zingales, L. (2009). The future of securities regulation. *Journal of Accounting Research, 47*(2), 391–425.

Zyskind, G., & Nathan, O. (2015, May). Decentralizing privacy: Using blockchain to protect personal data. In *2015 IEEE security and privacy workshops* (pp. 180–184). IEEE.

Printed in the USA
CPSIA information can be obtained
at www.ICGtesting.com
JSHW011434200624
65131JS00003B/14